Affective Maturity for Apostolic Effectiveness

Maureen Akabogu

Affective Maturity for Apostolic Effectiveness

A Handbook for Priests and Religious

Edizioni Sant'Antonio

Publisher:
Edizioni Sant'Antonio
is a trademark of
International Book Market Service Ltd., member of OmniScriptum Publishing Group
17 Meldrum Street, Beau Bassin 71504, Mauritius

Printed at: see last page
ISBN: 978-613-8-39251-4

Affective Maturity for Apostolic Effectiveness

A Handbook for Priests and Religious

Maureen Ogochukwu Akabogu, IHM

*In honour
of Archbishop Charles Heerey C.S.Sp (1829-1967)
Founder of the Religious Institute
of the Sisters of the Immaculate
Heart of Mary, Mother of Christ.*

ACKNOWLEDGEMENTS

Every book is born out of complimentary efforts; no book is a unilateral effort. Thus, I nurture a great deal of gratitude to all who contributed to the success of this book. Special thanks to all my friends, colleagues, and clients. Through them I gained many insights, and inspirations. I remain grateful for their contributions.

Special thanks to the following people for their enthusiastic support and encouragements spiritually, financially, academically, morally and otherwise. May God continue to shower his abundant blessings and graces upon them.

His Eminence, Francis Cardinal Arinze
His Grace, Most Rev. Dr. Valerian Okeke
His Lordship, Most Rev. Denis Isizoh
Very Rev. Fr. Prof. Bede Ukwuije, C.S. Sp
Rev. Fr. Augustine Okochi
Rev. Fr. Anthony Ezeugo
Rev. Mother Mary Claude Oguh, *IHM*
Sr. Mary Agnita Maduka, *IHM*
Sr. Mary Jerome Obiorah, *IHM*
Sr. Maria Philipeen Osei-Wusu, *IHM*
Sr. Maria Sapientia Ameke, *IHM*
Sr. Maria Amalachukwu Oguadimma, *IHM*
Sr. Geraldine Mariette Mgbemena, *IHM*
Prof. Antonino Urso
Prof. Teresa Doni
Dr Mrs Scholar Ezeodili

CONTENTS

10

12

PREFACE

It is a delight, a joy, to watch the performance of an expert organist, pianist or footballer. Such perfect control has been made possible by many years of consistent and disciplined practice. In a somewhat similar way, it is a blessing for the Church and society at the level of parish, diocese, religious congregation or other institution, to enjoy the services of a priest or religious brother or sister who has attained a high level of affective maturity in interpersonal relationships.

Such personnel of the Church have learned, under God's grace, to understand, control and direct emotions, to deal with basic attractions and fears, and, like the sun flower, to direct their heart towards Christ. For them, Jesus is the light, the sun, the centre of their loves and struggles and the one who gives unity, meaning and joy to their lives. They live for him, work for him and seek to reflect him and to draw souls to him. Such Christ-centeredness is particularly needed if priests and religious are to live the vocation to consecrated chastity with maturity, calm, credibility and apostolic fruitfulness.

This book by Sister Dr. Maureen O. Akabogu, I.H.M., Affective Maturity For Apostolic Effectiveness, will be found particularly useful by priests and consecrated people in the religious life and members of secular institutes. God gives the vocation and grace to virginity or celibacy. But the individual is expected to work with this grace. Saint Augustine says that "God created us without us, but he did not will to save us without us" (Sermon 169, 11, 13).

The Church in Nigeria in our times is particularly blessed with many young people who want to become priests or religious. Seminaries and novitiates are heavily populated. But if the Church is to rejoice that the Lord has not only multiplied the numbers of candidates, but also multiplied the joy of the Church (cf Is 9:3), then great attention is to be given to the formation of candidates. This book will be found particularly useful by seminary formators and religious congregations formation personnel, and indeed also by their superiors who have to take decisions regarding the affective maturity of their prospective members. I strongly recommend it.

+ Francis Card. Arinze
VATICAN CITY
17 February 2019

INTRODUCTION

The human heart can be likened to a sun flower that continually searches for light for its survival. Wherever the sun goes, the flower bends towards that direction. The human heart bends towards affection and nurturance. Affective maturity is a process of directing, structuring, and restructuring the human heart as it bends towards that universal need for love. It makes sure it is in the right direction, and that it acquires all the necessary principles for tackling and overcoming the obstacles on the road to the true Light for survival. This of course is a tedious and engaging task. There is always the crucible of struggle. Many experiences can disaffect the heart and block the process of its growth towards this maturity. Therefore, it is good to be patient with one's pace and observe the stride involved in the journey, to grasp the process and what it entails.

The increasing number of men and women with "intrinsically disordered" (*CCC 2357*) sexual tendencies both in the Church and in the society is a reality and quite challenging. News on the sexual misconduct of some Church ministers have rendered a good number of the faithful disgusted. There is no doubt it may have diminished the zeal of many in ecclesiastical affairs. This affects both the credibility and integrity of the Church. However, the Church has never ceased to provide adequate structures and programs she deemed sufficient at different times for the formation of her ministers. Nor has the Church ceased to offer insights on the best method of handling one's sexuality and related concepts within the sphere of celibate life. This notwithstanding, it is still evident that sometimes certain misconduct which portrays poor management of affection are recorded. A great pain indeed!

Celibacy is a gift and charism which priests of the Catholic Church in the Latin rite enjoy, by God's Grace. It is not as a result of the priests' spiritual or intellectual ability. According to St Paul, *we are only the earthenware jars that hold this treasure, to make it clear that such an overwhelming power comes from God and not from us* (2 Cor. 4:7). The same applies to all forms of consecrated life. While many priests and religious appreciate this rare gift of total self-giving, some understand it as a burden and an inhibition to full human maturity. Some even attribute the inappropriate behaviors of some Church ministers to mandatory celibacy. Some members argue that celibacy is not necessary for the sanctification of a religious and therefore should not be an obligation for the Latin rite, arguing that it is Church law and not God's law. Others argue that it is another form of modern slavery where people are deprived of their freedom, love, and other innate needs. This kind of argument can degenerate to a narrow way of thinking where some people think that purity is something outdated, celibacy a cross, virginity archaic and awkward and therefore should be abolished. However, neither priestly nor religious life is imposed on anyone. It has always been a free choice. At every stage of formation, the candidate writes an application to proceed to the next stage.

Worthy of note is that wherever there is a gift or treasure, there lies some difficulties associated with it. Attainment of affective maturity provides the key to understanding and handling the difficulties associated with this priceless treasure offered by God through the Church to a few individuals. While many people are interested in getting the paedophiles punished and dismissed, this book portrays more interest in helping priests and religious acquire the necessary skills to attain affective maturity. Only when one is affectively mature can she or he manage the great force of libido and eros, putting the force under control and channelling the energy more positively in life. Lack of affective maturity has crippled some priests and religious. To some, it has reduced their level of apostolic effectiveness.

The first chapter tries to understand the psychological structures and dynamics of the human person who is called to bear witness to the world. This is because the 'self' is both the subject and object of priestly and religious ministry. It discusses the effects of the psychological structures of the self in one's relational life. The question of integrating the two structures (ideal and actual self) remains a challenge to priests and religious. This is due to the unconscious influences in their lives. This inconsistency brings about some inner divisions and conflicts in their relational dimensions. However, one's positive attitudes and values are great aids to maintaining the required equilibrium of the self. The level of maturity in one's self-esteem, self-concept, self-awareness, and sexual self-awareness helps one to manage the conflicts arising from disunity between the ideal and the actual self.

The second chapter concentrates on the process of the development of the self. It exposes the self in its unitary form, the self as a thinking (cognitive domain) and feeling (affective domain) being. It emphasizes the need for integrating both the cognitive and affective domain of the person to obtain a holistic personality. Using the parameter of Piaget and Vygotsky, the chapter underscores the epigenetical process of cognitive development and the role of social interaction. It also stresses the fact that the type of attachment or bonding which a person receives as a child contributes a lot to affective development and maturity of the person.

The third chapter attempts a coherent understanding of the term 'affective maturity'. It exposes its principles as emotional regulation, self-regulation, psycho-social stability, psychosexual integration, healthy relationships, healthy self-esteem and the use of responsible freedom. Aware that there is a correlation between the level of affective maturity and apostolic effectiveness of priests and religious, the chapter emphasizes the need to adopt the principles and to develop them. Highlighting the fact that affective maturity does not imply being cold or indifferent, it reiterates the fact that affective maturity is a prerequisite for genuine interpersonal relationship. Since priests and religious are also social beings, it becomes also necessary for them for a better and more pleasant interaction in their ministry and apostolate. Psychosexual integration requires an opening up of oneself to another in love (both same-sex and heterosexual). Any form of genital intimacy of course does not form part of this. Running away from the opposite sex is a distortion of psychosexual integration and maturity.

The fourth chapter centers on the phenomenon of emotions, emphasizing its role as it gives meaning to one's actions and behaviors. It underlines the neutrality of emotions. While emotions in themselves have no moral judgment except when they are put into action, the chapter stresses the need for controlling these emotions and suggests possible and practical ways to do that. The fifth chapter opens another horizon to acquiring affective maturity through development of empathy, establishment of healthy relational boundaries, management of attractions, communication dynamics and conflict management. The last chapter centers on the art of obtaining affective maturity. Affective maturity is an art and therefore there is the need to learn the art. Through psychotherapy, resilience, and having recourse to a model like the Blessed Virgin Mary, one can sustain balance in his or her affective life.

Chapter One

THE PSYCHOLOGICAL STRUCTURE
OF THE HUMAN PERSON

This chapter focuses on the definition of self by exposing its psychological structure and content. Healthy relationship depends on the level of the knowledge of the self and the acceptance of the self. A clear understanding of self-concept, self-awareness, self-esteem, and self-efficacy underpin affective maturity and hence healthy interpersonal relationships. Knowledge of the content of the self, allows one to have an insight into what motivates one's actions, while knowledge of the structure of the self, helps to address the issue of the basic dialectical tensions. A sound development and sustenance of each sphere give rise to a holistic person with the capacity to complement others in daily activities, as well as being open to be complemented. While a distortion of any of the domains implies a dysfunctional person, who is inept in a relational context. This is because "it is the self that directs a person's behaviour"[1]. For once the self is disorganized, every relationship that it engages in automatically becomes disorganized.

The aim of this chapter is to help the reader have an objective knowledge of him/herself. This aids one to perceive oneself in a realistic manner as a psychological being who is open to self-transcendence. Since affective maturity is fundamental to the character formation of the human person, a clear understanding of this human person is important. Therefore, the chapter will proceed to define the self. The terms, self, ego, and human person are related in themselves but do not mean the same thing in the strict sense of the word. However, this book will make use of them interchangeably.

---

[1]   Cencini, Amaedo, and Alessandro Manenti. 2010. *Psychology and Formation: Structures and Dynamics*. Mumbai, India: Pauline Sisters, p. 278.

DEFINING THE 'SELF'

Defining the self is an uphill task. Attempt to do this is akin to describing God who is a mystery. The human person participates in this mystery. Many authors take different approaches to the definition of the self. However, the *self* here implies, the totality of the living organism of the human person, body and soul, incarnate spirit. That is, the self as the conscious entity, in the sense of having self-knowledge, a self-concept, and self-esteem; of being self-aware, self-critical; of feeling self-important; and of striving towards self-actualisation[2]. I intend here, the self that is not enslaved by the unconscious or the past, but the human person in the present. That is, the person that appreciates the present situation trusting God, remembers the past with gratitude to God and is ready to make amends for the future where it is necessary. In other words, the "self as the subject who actively experiences, perceives, feels, imagines, chooses, remembers or plans"[3]. This is the self that is called to love and to give oneself to God through the religious and priestly life; and who bears witness to Christ through apostolic ministry. Again, the physical aspect of the self is not neglected. Admittedly, the renowned author Ausubel highlights the physical aspect of the self. According to him, the appearance of the human person, the auditory image, kinesthetic sensations, and even tension is fundamental to the definition of the self[4]. This is the self that is concerned with beauty and aesthetics.

It is often difficult to differentiate between the *person* and the *self*. Nevertheless, 'person' is synonymous with the 'self', but there is a clear difference. Psychologically, every person has a self. Therefore, the self is simply defined as one's personality which is always

---

[2] LeDoux, Joseph. 2003. *Synaptic Self: How Our Brains Become Who We Are*. NY: Penguin, p. 27.

[3] Gordon, Chad, and Kenneth. J. Gergen. 1968. *The Self in Social Interaction*. Vol. I. NY: John Willey and Sons, p. 33.

[4] Ausubel, David P. 1959. *Theory and Problems of Child Development*. NY: Grune and Stratton, p. 273.

in the process of maturation. It encircles the totality of a being, including behavioural potentials and abilities. It also includes in its entirety one's temperament, value system, goals, and preferences[5]. In this sense, one cannot compare the self of a neophyte with that of an adult. The emphasis lies more in the qualitative difference of both selves. The self can also be understood as the synthesizing principle of all the mechanisms and activities which the human person engages in. In this case, the self becomes the pivotal agent which functions in a specific manner as to harmonise and unify the personality and maintain its integrity. When understood as a unifying principle, the self becomes an abstract which is undefinable.

Notwithstanding this conclusion, this chapter will attempt to describe the self in four terms: self-awareness, self-concept, self-esteem, and self-efficacy.

a. Self-Awareness: The Primary Task

This means many things to different people. It is "usually regarded as self-focused attention, selective processing of information about the self"[6]. This selective processing is prerequisite for the development of the self-concept. Self-awareness helps in the processing of important personal information. It entails people's ability to have access to the information about themselves. This information can be either from the psyche or from the heart. It helps in the processing of data. Self-awareness is mainly achieved through the process of socialisation, participation in religious, cultural, and social programs. Through reflected appraisals, feedback from others, self-perception, arousal states both physiological, biochemical and environmental distinctiveness[7].

---

[5] Leary, Mark R., and June P. Tangney. 2003. *Handbook of Self and Identity*. NY: Guilford Press, p. 6-7.

[6] Leary, Mark R., and June P. Tangney. 2003, p. 183.

[7] Taylor, Shelley E., Ann L. Peplau, and David O. Sears. 2006. *Social Psychology*. Twelfth Edition. Upper Saddle River, NJ: Pearson Education International, p. 100.

Self-awareness occurs with the conscious rumination and reflection on one's actual self in the here and now. In doing this, the past experiences are not left aside. In fact, it is the evaluation or the comparisons between one's real life and one's desired and expected life in relation to one's set goals. In this sense, self-awareness can be objective. The result of this comparison sometimes brings along some dialectical tensions and some knowledge of one's shortcomings. This leads to the experience of negative emotions. Nevertheless, one of the advantages of this dialectic is that it may compel the self to work towards the desired goal. One can also be aware of her private self (one's feelings, thoughts, and attitudes) and public self (how other people see the person). While private self is mainly oriented towards growth by evaluating one's standards and value system, the public self is oriented towards presenting oneself positively to others – *fare bella figura*.

Self-awareness is the primary task along the pathway of affective maturity. Being aware means being attuned to the present moment, that is being conscious. When a person is self-aware, it enables that person to recognize his or her shadows and to integrate it as part of his or her identity. For example, one who does not recognize his or her shadow of aggressiveness, will be surprised at his or her explosion even in public as he or she quarrels. While the person who recognizes this shadow will handle situations that may provoke quarrelling in a mature manner. Self- knowledge instils in people inner sense of security and self-assurance which gives depth in one's character.

b. Self-Concept: The Invisible Mover

Self-concept is merely the perception of oneself. That is, how one views himself or herself concerning the environment. It refers to the concrete beliefs which individual holds to be true as observed in concrete life. The content of this belief may be either abstract or tangible. It can also be evaluative when it concerns people's character or intelligence. In this sense, it becomes simply "an abstraction of the essential and distinguishing characteristics of the self that differentiate an individual's "selfhood" from the environment and other selves"[8]. Suffice it to say, that it is the essence of a person. No two individuals can have the same self-concept. It is what makes individual A different from individual B. Self-concept is not innate but acquired and is developed through childhood. It is influenced by nature and nurture. One can always reshape and restructure one's self-concept to adapt to the present context. One can also change one's perception or idea regarding many concepts, ranging from physical, spiritual, mental, emotional and relational tendencies. It implies that self-concept is not static since one's ideas are liable to change in time and space. Mood and environment can as well alter the already established concept. There is always room for evaluation and modification of self-concept.

Self-concept is like an inner push or pull towards maturity since it is multi-dimensional. The way a person perceives himself or herself and the beliefs associated with this perception has a lot to contribute in one's attitude and general functioning. If a priest perceives himself as never succeeding in his ministry or a nun perceives herself as not capable of handling her apostolate, automatically both will experience anxiety in their lifestyle. And the result will be spending energy to avoid failure, rather than investing energy to succeed. But if both perceive themselves as capable of facing the challenges associated with their ministry and apostolate, they will be more motivated and confident in executing their duties. Undoubtedly, a balanced self-concept contributes greatly to one's self-image as it helps mainly in the psychosocial development and stability of the human person. This is because it strengthens the skill to collaborate with others in the social setting; strengthens one's competence and awakens the person to emotional consciousness of one's present state of life.

It is important that one's self-concept corresponds to reality and not be attached only to the ideals. This is mainly observed in the case of neurotics or narcissistic personality whose perception of reality

---

[8]   Ausubel, David P. 1959, p. 273.

24

is distorted. Indeed, some individuals are confused and uncertain about both their cognitive and emotional states. The question of incongruency of one's self-concept does not lead to growth, it rather delays the person's maturity since one is acting based on a false self. However, depending on situations, one can be helped by others to maintain congruency in one's perception of the real self.

Furthermore, self-awareness is pivotal to self-concept. Hence, self-concept includes only those characteristics of which the individual is aware and believes that he exercises control over them[9]. It follows that intrapsychic experiences do not form part of the self-concept since they are not always conscious. There must be that awareness and ability to communicate one's concept. Shadows (the aspect of one's personality which is often repressed because it conflicts with one's ideals and principles) and unconsciousness do not form part of the self-concept. The ability to observe and identify one's self-concept is a basic step and procedure to formation in affective maturity.

c. Self-Esteem: The Unconscious Assurance

Self-esteem is a definitive part of the human person. It conditions one lot and contributes to one's predisposition to actions and behaviours. It is highly subjective in an evaluation. The evaluation centres on an individual's perception of the private self or subjective self. Worthy of note is that a person can have an inaccurate perception and evaluation of oneself. In this case, one may have either an inflated ego or a deflated one. None of this is good for proper functioning in the society. For this reason, it is necessary to differentiate between two types of self-esteem: contingent self-esteem and true self-esteem. Contingent self-esteem refers to "feelings about oneself that result matching some standard of excellence or living up

---

[9] Rogers, Carl R. 1951. *Client-Centered Therapy. Its Current Practice, Implications, and Theory.* Cambridge, MA: Houghton Mifflin Company, p. 498.

to some interpersonal or intrapsychic expectations"[10]. In this case, success is the criteria for high self-esteem. Therefore, self-esteem becomes transitive and situational. Hence, a priest or a nun feels a high sense of worth only when he or she succeeds in his or her apostolate or when he or she meets up with the desired set goals.

For people with contingent self-esteem, "belonging to a class" and "meeting up" is of great priority to them. These are the group of people who prefer 'doing' rather than 'being'. Mainly, competitions and comparisons spur them for actions and behaviours. Their primary force for actions comes from the external (social class; competitions and comparisons), rather than the internal (value system and personal conviction). The fact of this force from outside implies a kind of readiness and willingness to adopt any type of means to achieve the desired goal. People in this category are success oriented at all cost. Narcissism plays an underlying role in contingent self-esteem.

The second type of self-esteem is the true self-esteem. It is centered on a real and solid sense of self. An individual with true self-esteem values himself or herself even amid failures and disappointments in life. It is based on the reality principle where one appreciates oneself for who he or she is. In this case, one's self-worth is not dependent or limited to the desired and achieved success. One believes that he or she is ever precious and valuable before God and other people. Although people with high true self-esteem have ambitions, inspirations and goals to achieve in life, their inability to reach their desired target does not destabilize them. Here lies the major difference between contingent and true self-esteem. Those with true self-esteem put in their whole energy both internally and externally to succeed and are happy when they succeed. Nevertheless, when the reverse is the case, they may feel pain and disappointed, but their sense of worth neither diminishes nor fluctuates. It remains intact.

---

[10] Deci, Edward L., and Richard M. Ryan. 1995. "Human Autonomy: The Basis for True Self-Esteem". Pp. 31-46 in *Efficacy, Agency, and Self-Esteem*, edited by M. H. Kernis. NY: Plenum Press, p. 32

26

Those with true self-esteem put in their whole energy both internally and externally to succeed and are happy when they succeed. Nevertheless, when the reverse is the case, they may feel pain and disappointed, but their sense of worth neither diminishes nor fluctuates. It remains intact.

True self-esteem does not cancel realism. One who fails is bound to feel pain, but with the understanding that failure does not define him or her. Failure at that moment was just a transitory experience. It is for this that those with true self-esteem are generally unwavering and resilient in the face of failure. They are emotionally and affectively stable and as such are not easily influenced or persuaded by other people. They "have no conflict between wanting and obtaining success and approval since they react positively to a happy and successful life; through consistent and stable self-concept and self-enhancement oriented"[11]. Therefore, a healthy self-esteem is an antidote to anxiety and depression. This is because a person with high self-esteem has a strong sense of social inclusion and social acceptance. He or she has internal freedom and feels happy.

The author Baumeister maintains that self-esteem has a very powerful influence on human cognition, motivation, emotion, and behaviour. In his effort to explain the concept of self-esteem, he outlined some of the characteristics of those with low self-esteem. He believes that those with low self-esteem are often more reactive to external stimulus in the social context and are more conservative in their attitude towards others[12]. They evaluate themselves as inept, unskilled, and even unlovable by those around them. This inner insecurity pushes them to read demeaning into every event. They tend towards receiving information about themselves which is in

---

[11] Hogg, Michael A., and Graham M. Vaughan. 2011. *Social Psychology*. Sixth Edition. London, U.K.: Pearson Press. 2011, p. 137.

[12] Baumeister, Roy F. 1993. *Self-Esteem. The Puzzle of Low Self-Regard*. NY: Plenum Press, p. 3-10.

line with their negative and maladaptive thinking and behaviours. Instead of being active in any social event, they ordinarily prefer passiveness. Rather than utilizing and appreciating their God-given talents and placing it at people's service, they spend much time practicing how to subdue those talents so as not to risk failure in their effort to make use of them.

Those with low self-esteem have "lighter skin". They are less resilient in the face of difficult experiences. With this, they are more disturbed with some threats (both real and imagined). Often, low self-esteem is confused with humiliation or abasement[13] in the spiritual setting. Nevertheless, those with low self-esteem wish to succeed, to love and be loved, to exhibit some of their hidden talents, but these desires seem very difficult to actualize in their lives. Because they wrongly interpret their desires to be a very difficult task, their major target in most of their concrete experiences is to avoid failure, humiliation, rejection, and other unpleasant outcomes. Since they have known the pains of failure, they are very sensitive to that. All their energy and efforts are therefore channelled towards protecting their delicate and fragile ego from their supposed hostile outside world. They lack the emotional resources to cope with distressing outcomes.

Consequently, they lean toward neutral self-presentations. Low self-esteem is not necessarily self-rejection or self-hatred, it is instead the fact of accepting and portraying oneself in a neutral and sometimes negative manner. It is a matter of wrong perception of the self, a wrong perception of one's identity. They often have bias and inaccurate perception about themselves. Sometimes purely erroneous perception. In most cases they are not willing to give up these inaccurate perceptions. Only when they are open to change can they modify their self-esteem.

---

[13] Abasement in the words of Rulla implies, "to submit to external force. To accept injury, blame, criticism, punishment. To surrender. To become resigned to fate. To admit inferiority, error, wrongdoing, or defeat. To confess and atone. To blame, belittle, or mutilate the self. To seek and enjoy pain, punishment, illness and misfortune. Cf. Rulla, L.M. 2004. *Anthropology of the Christian Vocation, Volume I*. Gregorian University Press, p. 464.

Research has shown that increase in self-esteem is likely to occur during time of transition, for example, a from the junior seminary to the senior seminary; from postulate to novitiate; transition as a temporarily professed to a finally professed sister; moving from one parish to the other etc. All these provide adequate opportunities to meet people of different understanding with different approach to life in their different worldviews. A healthy person will always re-evaluate his or her life before embarking on significant life transitions.

d. Self-Efficacy: The Confident Guide

This refers to personal beliefs about one's abilities "to organize and execute the courses of action required to produce given attainments"[14]. Planning is always less tasking than executing. A self-efficient person is therefore, one who believes he or she can plan, organise and execute effectively already planned actions and projects. However, this belief does not always produce a positive outcome. Self-efficiency touches the belief system of a person. A clear concept of one's self-efficacy is pivotal to the formation of the self especially in affective sphere. Lack of this makes individuals more suggestible than others. It makes one vulnerable, dependent and prone to failure. It leads to either overestimation or underestimation of the self.

> *Unless people believe they can produce desired effects by their actions, they have little incentive to undertake activities or to persevere in the face of difficulties.*
>
> MATUMOTO, DAVID

In the strict sense of the word, self-efficacy is not about competence, the emphasis is on the "belief" in one's aptitude to exercise certain skills. Competency has to do with knowledge and technical ability, which include both cognitive constructions and behavioural elements. There is no moral attachment to these beliefs, they can be

---

[14] Bandura, Albeit. 1997. *Self-Efficacy: The Exercise of Control*. NY: Freeman, p. 3.

accurate or inaccurate, positive, or negative. It concentrates on the present moment[15]. The core belief implied here is the foundation of human motivation, performance accomplishments, and emotional well-being. "Unless people believe they can produce desired effects by their actions, they have little incentive to undertake activities or to persevere in the face of difficulties"[16]. Those with high self-efficacy approach difficulties as challenges to overcome and not as obstacles to be avoided. They see difficult tasks as opportunities to expand their technical skills and are open to learning.

THE COMPONENTS OF THE *SELF*

The self functions at three levels: psycho-physiological, psycho-social, and rational-spiritual level[17]. The first level of the psychic life which is psycho-physiological centres on providing immediate satisfaction for a happy life. Here the basic need to satisfy hunger, or to gain shelter becomes indispensable for subjective well-being of people. Any deficiency on this level brings about unhappiness and distress. Intrinsically, the biological process at the primary level pushes one to go in search of fulfilment of this aspect. The second level which is psycho-social concentrates on the human person as a social animal who has the need to be in communion with God and the people. The principal drive here is the quest for completion, since no individual feels complete in him/herself. Here interpersonal relationship becomes a necessary concept. The last level which is the rational-spiritual is "linked to the need to know the truth, and the related human capacity to grasp the nature of things, abstracting it from sensual data"[18]. It is at this level that we talk of self-transcendence. That is, when individuals are willing to go beyond their human nature in search for the Creator.

---

[15] Leary, Mark R., and June P. Tangney. 2003, p. 219-220.

[16] Matsumoto, David. 2009. *The Cambridge Dictionary of Psychology*. NY: Cambridge University Press. p.470.

[17] Nuttin G. 1967. *Psicoanalisi e Personalita*, Paoline, Alba, pp. 290-295.

[18] Cencini, Amaedo, and Alessandro Manenti. 2010, p. 23.

Willed by choice, it is the duty of the individual not to exclude any of the levels. The three levels of psychic life must be in harmony for maturity to occur. There must be the conscious search for equilibrium, both interior and exterior. Interdependence among the three levels is vital.

The components of the self are what determines the level of operation at a given time. They are the background of living and operating a healthy life. They explain what motivates and pushes a person into certain behaviours. The question "why" a person is attracted to particular behaviour and not the other is explained in the components of the self. They include: the needs, the values, and attitudes. We explain them briefly.

a. Need: The Natural Urge that Persist

The Oxford dictionary of psychology defines need as "lack of something that is required for survival; a motivational state resulting from the lack of something that an organism requires or desires… "[19]. The definition stresses the crucial nature of the need for survival. Needs are indispensable for growth and development, especially the biological needs. It is also a drive or a strong desire to accomplish what one feels vital for existence. Needs carry along with them some psychic energy which pushes one to act, but which must not necessarily produce action. It is merely a tendency. So that need is not enough to produce actions. It rather disposes a person for action. For example, the need for success disposes a student to consistent and serious studies. There is always a space for decision making in support of the need in question. It exposes one to act in the present moment. It is the will that decides the execution of the strong pull of need.

Needs are innate in man, without which man will be more passive than active in the society. In fact, without the needs the

---

[19] Colman, Andrew M. 2009. *Oxford Dictionary of Psychology*. NY: Oxford University Press, p. 495.

human person will be incapable of formulating thoughts or gestures. This is due to the great psychic energy which they produce. With this fundamental orientation, man is faced with the practical and technical aptness to seek for adaptable means of satisfying the needs. In other words, the need must be channelled since it has a senseless route.

Behind the idea of the need is the unconscious desire for the "homeostatic principle of reduction of tension"[20]. It is merely to supply for a deficiency even when the deficiency is unreal and imagined. There is always the quest to discover a suitable gratification. This is merely in the aspect of physiological needs like hunger.

The renowned Psychologists Murray goes deeper to enumerate some psychological needs which chain and impede maturity and authentic spiritual growth. The dissonant needs (abasement, aggression, exhibition, sexual gratification, succourance, etc.) are more complex, influential and more difficult to control, while the consonant needs (affiliation, knowledge, domination, autonomy, counteraction, etc.) are less harmful. Nevertheless, needs cannot be reduced only to the gratification of the primary process (pleasure principle), since one is not determined to act by its impulse. There is the space and possibility of yielding to the secondary process (reality principle).

b. Values

Values differ from needs for the fact that they are not innate in the human person. They are not *given*, one acquires values. Values are mainly virtues. Before the acquisition is the strong attraction of these values. It is this strong attraction that pushes one to imitate, to emulate and to replicate an attitude. Values have cognitive, affective, and conative elements. On the level of cognition, one must have an intellectual knowledge of what attracts him or her. When this is known, it evokes some emotions. But the conative element plays

---

[20] Cencini, Amaedo, and Alessandro Manenti. 2010, p. 93.

more roles. Hence, it is not enough to know about the value or to feel the relevance of the value, more important is that the value is transformed into concrete action. The person does not stop at the contemplation or feeling but moves into action to practice the value[21]. Furthermore, values have some vital functions and contributions to the moral development of the self. First, they attach a sense of identity to the person. In this case, one's value defines the person. Since value is that ideal or standard which the ego has consistently identified with in the positive sense of the word. Consequently, it shields the ego from being determined and ruled by the pleasure principle, and therefore helps the ego to maintain a new form of life which is in consonant with the strong attraction of the value. It serves as a motivational force, just like a need.

Values can also serve as one's paradigm. In this case, it becomes like a road map for one's journey. This is because it motivates and justifies one's behaviour and serves as standards for judging people, actions, and situations. It therefore regulates one's life.

The self can possess transcendental values either in the form of moral or religious values. In this case a person is expected to exercise responsible freedom in his or her behaviours. When one possesses transcendental values, one's actions spring up from one's free will. While moral value affects the essence of the self and is more pragmatic and may serve as a yardstick for the worth and dignity of the human person, religious value refers mainly to one's personal relationship with God. Religious value is mainly achieved in religion. However, one must integrate both moral and religious values to develop good behaviours.

c. Attitudes

Attitude is derived from the Latin word *aptus*, meaning 'fit and ready for action'. The definition implies a certain type of physicality,

---

[21] Cencini, Amaedo, and Alessandro Manenti. 2010, p. 125-126.

something that is observable. But it is more than that. Some underlying processes, though not observable contribute to the formulation of one's attitudes. The degree of positive and negative affect with the object, determines the attitude that one exhibits[22]. An attitude is a predisposition. However, every predisposition or preference is not an attitude. Some predispositions are momentary and therefore do not last. An attitude must be lasting, an enduring disposition are what constitute an attitude. Suffice it to say that the disposition must be consistent and habitual. Although some attitudes are hereditary, some are acquired, just like the values.

As in the case of values, cognition plays important role both in forming and sustaining some positive attitudes, but the affective part cannot be underestimated as well. An attitude can still last even if the cognitive element is lacking. For example, in the stereotypic attitude, if at the cognitive level individual A thinks and holds that individual B is wicked, the affective element carries it out through a feeling of repulsion or coldness towards the individual in question. Often the affective dominates and clouds reasoning in attitudinal formation. The affective memory plays a significant role here so that once the individual experiences an unpleasant attitude, subsequent episodes become more intense.

Furthermore, attitude can be positive or negative feeling about a person or an issue. It concerns the preferences of individual persons. Though the influence of a group may affect the formation of attitudes, the intrapsychic processes play more role. The community or the society to which a person belongs also contributes to the formation of attitudes. Upholding and sustaining the group's identity and integrity is often the primary reason. Social approval and the need for affiliation are the underlying unconscious motivations to form certain attitudes. The influence of attitude on behaviour can be automatic or deliberate.

---

[22] Hogg, Michael A., and Graham M. Vaughan. 2011, p. 148-149.

THE STRUCTURES OF THE SELF

The word 'structure' here refers to "a system which represents the laws, or the organisational properties of a totality seen as a whole; these properties explain why this and not another content is realized"[23]. There is no ideal structure, neither is there a fixed structure, for in the complexity of the self, there are different elements which produce both internal and external forces that pull the self to act. In the structure of the self is also found some dynamics which oppose themselves and which sometimes are out of one's control. The more they oppose themselves, the more the self is disorganized and tends towards pathology. The more they are in harmony, the more the self is consolidated and develops into an integral whole. The place of these structures help in the construction and establishment of one's stable identity.

Rulla structurally divides the self into two: the actual self and the ideal self. These selves have contrasting characteristics[24]. They have different lines of development as well. While the actual self is based on the development of the id and ego, the ideal self- depends on the level of the superego which deals with the moral development of the person. There is always a conflict between the two structures. Operating strictly from one sphere would suggest a form of disorganization of the self.

a. The Actual Self

The actual self simply means what one is at present, in the here and now: how a person behaves in real life. According to Rulla, the actual self as a structure is the self that "grows towards self-transcendence or resists growth, consciously or unconsciously. This is the self as transcended"[25]. Primarily, the actual self desires to go

---

[23] Cencini, Amaedo, and Alessandro Manenti. 2010, p.165-172.

[24] Rulla, Luigi M. 2004. *Anthropology of Christian Vocation*. Vol. 1. Rome, Italy: Gregorian University Press, p. 167.

[25] Rulla, Luigi M. 2004, p. 167.

beyond the natural instincts and determinism in search of God but is influenced by some unconscious forces which inhibit this desire. It can also decide to yield to the natural instincts and live in the world of pleasures and desires. The self here is somehow aware of its behaviours but may not also be fully aware of its dynamics due to the presence of some unconscious needs.

The actual self has three components: the manifest self, the latent self, and the social self. Manifest self is equivalent to the self-concept. It is what the person knows and believes about oneself. The latent self is those characteristics which a person possesses and is unaware of them (needs, attitudes, emotions). They influence one's conduct. The social self is what a person thinks he or she is according to the interpretation and judgment of others. The actual self also contains the 'world of desire', which includes the world of fantasy, illusion, imagination and the world as one perceives it to be. This entails many questions and confusion by the individual who sometimes desires to understand many things about one's life. Nevertheless, there are no fixed limits to what the self can desire.

b. The Ideal Self

This is the self which in its motivational structure, strives and aspires to grow increasingly in its ideals of self-transcendence. Here the self operates at the level of consciousness[26]. The self here goes beyond just self-realisation. It tends more to acquire self-transcendental values. The ideals here are made up of both natural and self-transcendental values. Here the person willingly wants to adopt these values. The person is neither persuaded nor constrained to absorb these values, but there is rather the willingness to do that. There is internal and external freedom. The ideal self helps in the organisation of interdependent motivational forces. It is also combination of personal ideals and institutional or societal ideals. The institutional ideals depend on how the individual perceives it[27]. When perceived

---

[26] Rulla, Luigi M. 2004, p. 167.

[27] Cencini, Amaedo, and Alessandro Manenti. 2010, p. 175.

positively, it moves the individual into active expression of the desire to meet up with the expected standard of life. The person moves towards a conscious actualization of a meaningful life.

When there is a discrepancy between the ideal self and the real self, there is a dialectic. Self-discrepancies may produce strong emotions. This has a psychological impact on the person. It can generate dejection-related emotions and sometimes leads to depression.

Chapter Two

DEVELOPMENT OF THE SELF

Development entails a change in the quality of any organism. Nevertheless, all bodily changes are not development. The many potentials, which the human person has acquired from birth are actualised gradually through the process of evolution. Imoda concurs with this that, "development, as far as it is a progressive emergence of operative forms, ever more expressive of the potentials characterising the person, shows itself to be a series of changes which involve the very essence of the human person"[28]. In any development of a living organism, there is a systematic and sometimes visible changes in the life of the organism. It is this that finally leads to maturation. Development of the self involves the cognitive, affective, and conative processes. To have a wholesome and mature development of the self includes also forms of interpersonal relationships.

Development of the self is therefore an accidental change which does not affect the substance of the individual. The self has in potency all that it takes to develop into an integrated person, except for a pathological disorder which disrupts and limits the level of development.

COGNITIVE DEVELOPMENT AND FUNCTIONING OF THE SELF

The primary difference between man and animal is man's capacity for abstract thinking, logic, and human reasoning. This forms the essence of human experience. Cognition refers to all aspects of mental life, including the content and the process. It includes all

---

[28] Imoda, Franco. 2007. *Human Development. Psychology and Mystery*. Leuven, Belgium: Peeters, p. 103.

forms of concepts, facts, propositions, and memories. Healthy cognitive processes aid one to understand and interpret the world in a constructive manner[29]. Cognitive development is the pattern or way a child learns, understands, interprets, memorizes, and processes information. A healthy development of this domain helps the child to develop the capacity to multitask, coordinate many things together, and work in both structured and unstructured ways. It also aids one to make reasonable decisions as well as harmonise impulses and the instinctive nature. Otherwise, the child becomes poor in social performance with low intelligent quotient. Children who have less trauma and negative experience develop high and adequate cognition.

The concept of intelligence is pivotal to the development of cognition. All types of intelligence help in the development of the self and adaptation of this self. For example, interpersonal intelligence and emotional intelligence help more in community life. For intelligence is that fundamental process which enables an organism to adapt appropriately to an environment. This adaptation implies that the organism can cope with the difficulties of its immediate situation in an environment.

PIAGET AND VYGOTSKY ON THE COGNITIVE DEVELOPMENT OF THE SELF

Children learn more complicated cognitive structures with age. Their pattern of thought become more organised and more adaptable both in their private and public life as they mature in life. Contrary to some philosophers who believe that infants have some inborn knowledge or ideas about reality, Piaget contends that "they actively construct new understandings of the world based on their own experiences"[30]. This, they do by assimilating specific and ob-

---

[29] Gerrig, Richard J., and Phillip G. Zimbardo. 2010. *Psychology and Life*. Nineteenth Edition. Boston, MA: Pearson, p. 233.

[30] Schaffer, David R., and Katherine Kipp. 2010, *Developmental Psychology: Childhood and Adolescence*. Eight Edition. Belmont, VA: Wadsworth Cenage Learning, p. 54.

servable concrete experiences. They revise specific schemes with time as experiences contradict the already existing ones. It is an epigenetic stage as each stage builds on the previous one. According to Piaget, four major stages of cognitive development are necessary for a healthy development of a person: sensorimotor, preoperational, concrete operations and formal operations[31]. There is a sequential passage through the stages by all children.

At sensorimotor stage (birth to 2 years), the infant makes use of both sensory and motor capabilities to explore and learn more about themselves and the environment. The significant development here is that of object permanence. In the preoperational stage (2-7years), the child begins to use symbolism in the representation and understanding of different aspects of life. At the third stage (7 to 11 or 12 years), there are the concrete operations. In the last stage (11-12 years and above) comes the formal operations. As the child grows into an adolescent, he develops the capacity for logic and more abstract thinking. The ability for some hypothetical reasonings also becomes appreciable. They learn to be more systematic and apply deductive reasoning[32]. Piaget's theory of cognitive development explains the processes through which a child develops cognitively. For him intelligence and cognition are not a fixed or pre-determined trait, but rather a process which occurs because of the influence of nature and the environment where the individual grows.

On the other hand, Vygotsky stresses the fundamental role of social interaction in the development of cognition. In fact, the community is a prominent place and a vital factor for the development of cognition according to the author. Cognitive development cannot be complete without reference to the social and cultural context within which it is embedded. Therefore, cognitive development is a result of interpersonal relationship as there is intermingling of ideas, experiences and facts. He sustains that it is difficult and rare for all the children to go through the same processes as proposed by Piaget

---

[31]   Schaffer, David R., and Katherine Kipp. 2010. p. 55.

[32]   Schaffer, David R., and Katherine Kipp. 2010, p. 55.

40

in cognitive growth. In his socio-cultural theory, he believes that children internalise and replicate many cultural values which they inherit from their parents and caregivers. This is mainly through the process of cooperation with their elders and through observation and imitation. It is obvious that culture and the social context are vital for intellectual growth in the theory of Vygotsky. Children's mental development is closely linked to their way of life (culture), though with certain variations. In this, context is crucial to cognitive development.

AFFECTIVE DEVELOPMENT OF THE SELF

Affect is closely related to emotion, but it is not the same thing. Most psychologists use affect to simply refer to the observable aspect of emotion. Affect swings depending on one's emotional state. The affective domain includes physiological, cognitive, and behavioural processes related to emotion. Emotion is at the root of the affective domain. It gives meaning and vitality to interpersonal experiences. A mature approach to managing of one's emotions give rise to affective maturity. That is, the capacity of an individual to manage his affectivity freely and responsibly and acquiring the appropriate ways of expressing them in the presence of the other. This capacity is a gradual process, like new layers of an onion, which build upon the previous ones, until they all become a single mature onion. Anything can arouse our emotion. The concept of self which one develops is a dynamic factor in emotional responses. If one feels secure, loved, and worthy; if one's basic needs are met, his emotional reactions are more likely to be constructive. If his needs are thwarted, his emotions are negative[33]. The type of attachment behaviour which people experience during their childhood contributes a lot to their level of affective maturity in the future.

---

[33] Harold, Bernard. W. 1971. *Adolescent Development*. Scranton, PA: Intext Educational Publishers, p. 169-170.

THE ROLE OF ATTACHMENT BEHAVIOUR IN AFFECTIVE DOMAIN

The development of the affective domain of a person depends on the level of attachment and bonding which a child receives from the mother or the caregiver at the early years. Although, it does not imply that individual differences in attachment processes are deterministic of later development. Attachment behaviours do not determine the future life of an individual, strictly speaking. Otherwise, we would fall into the net of the psychoanalytic school of thought. However, the authors discovered empirically that there is a correlation and some meaningful associations with that. The initial relationship between the child and the mother helps in the future social relationships. When a child feels secure, "it contributes to the regulation of affect, the establishment of other social relationships, and the child's negotiation of subsequent developmental tasks"[34].

The issue of attachment begins very early as soon as the baby is born. Attachment behaviours vary from cuddling, smiling, caressing, breastfeeding, and the like. Smiling promotes attachment because it maintains the proximity of the caretaker. The infant develops an intense attachment to the mother or whoever gives immediate attention to her needs[35]. Attachment is essential throughout life process. It develops gradually, from a child who wants to be with the mum always, cuddled, to an adult who wants to be perceived as an autonomous entity and experience life with less anxiety. It is a profound and lasting connection or bond that is established between a child and the mother or a caregiver during the first years of life. It is an ongoing reciprocal love where both the child and the mother are involved. Attachment creates a disposition on the part of the child for the essential trust which is very helpful for future affective and emotional dealings. Secure attachment is needed for the development of the affect.

---

[34] Belsky, Jay., and Teresa Nezworski. 1998. *Clinical Implications of Attachment*. NJ: Lawrence Erbaum Associates Publishers, p. 4-5.

[35] Crain, William. 2005. *Theories of Development: Concepts and Applications*. NY: Pearson Education, p. 48-53.

A child with a secure attachment from the early months of birth develops the capacity for being positive. He or she grows up with perception and feelings of being loved and accepted. Such a child trusts in the good which the environment and people around have to offer. Whereas those babies with insecure attachment have negative feelings. They perceive the environment and people around as a threat, object of torture and dislike. Hence, they cannot trust because they feel unloved, not appreciated, and unwanted. This in effect leads to attachment disorders. Attachment disorders in effect lead to emotional and affective disorders, antisocial practices, and the like. In short, insecure attachments at the early stage is a severe issue. It makes one vulnerable since those mothers or caregivers fail to establish "an integrative self-organisational process"[36]. Secure attachments, on the other hand, from either caregivers or parents are the one that enhance all round growth and development of the self. By adolescence, the attachment system develops fully. Gradually, the cognitive and emotional advances of adolescent age, allows the person to reflect and modify his or her states of mind regarding attachment[37]. With time, adolescents de-idealise parents and understand them more as having both good and bad qualities. With this, there is no danger of identity diffusion and object constancy. They can interpret their inconsistencies and discrepancies as challenges of life and are therefore prepared to face the reality.

INFLUENCE OF NATURE AND NURTURE ON COGNITIVE AND AFFECTIVE FUNCTIONING OF THE SELF

Nature is the genetic heritage which a person gets from both parents from the time of conception. This extends throughout life. Many things are genetically inherited and cannot be changed; hence they manifest themselves through phenotype, which is the external charac-

---

[36] Siegel, Daniel J. 1999. *The Developing Mind: How Relationships and the Brain Interact to Shape Who We Are*. NY: Guildford Press, p. 314.

[37] Bowlby, John E. 1979. *The Making and Breaking of Affectional Bonds*. London, U.K.: Tavistock, p. 420.

teristics. These biological inherited tendencies and abilities manifest themselves in the later life of the individual. From early childhood, individuals begin to form an idea of the self, having feelings of self-worth. As already mentioned, if one's needs are met and one is satisfied, the person believes the world is friendly as well as the people around him or her. What others think of the child helps the child to form his or her self-concept. For example, if people say one is handsome, the person believes this, and it raises his or her self-esteem and self-worth. While acknowledging the great importance of nature versus nurture for development of the human person, the process of these influences in producing developmental change should also not be neglected. In the canalisation process, genes prevent or reduce the rate of development. Often, the environment has very little to contribute to the development as it is a natural process that an infant must undergo.

Nurture means more than physical care and love, although it certainly includes these essentials. It is the environmental factors that surround the individual from birth to death since at any moment, everyone exists within a given space. Nurture conveys the idea of protection as well as stimulation of the child. Children desire and need nurture. Often children in the homeless or adopted babies, suffer from lack of nurture, as a result, they have little capacity for relationships and have difficulty in trusting people. For, because they did not experience feelings of being loved, they cannot love in return and as such will need therapy to come out of this block.

PSYCHOLOGICAL SEPARATION OF THE SELF

As mentioned earlier, at the root of affective life is the type of attachment and bonding which an infant had. Whether one receives a secure or insecure attachment or bonding; there comes a time when there is need to leave this attachment figure. At some point in life, one must be independent and believe that he or she exists as a private body and assume full responsibility of taking care of himself or herself. So that an adult will understand in clear terms that he or she is responsible for his or her development.

44

> *People who are psychologically separated are free from the compulsion of repeating the feeling and the thought pattern of their primary caregivers or significant other in their lives. Possessing a psychologically separated self, renders one internally free, and enables one to think and feel clearly and objectively without inner inhibitions.*

The level of developmental progress depends on the much an individual is involved in the process. One does not need to be dependent on another for the achievement of his or her purposes in life. There is the need for one to claim autonomy from the principal caregivers or caretakers, abandoning even their habitual injunctions. Therefore, psychological separation of the self is simply about breaking patterns of attachment and nesting, otherwise it turns to be a repeated cycle which becomes a habit.

People who are psychologically separated are free from the compulsion of repeating the feeling and the thought pattern of their primary caregivers or significant other in their lives. Possessing a psychologically separated self, renders one internally free, and enables one to think and feel clearly and objectively without inner inhibitions. Ultimately, it disposes one to attach oneself to the Transcendent. Complete and absolute psychological separation is never possible. Often and on, we are attracted to people, fall in and out of love. But, it is to believe that we are the architects of our lives, the sole master. This does not imply lack of confusion sometimes, but that one is conscious of his or her integrity. It also implies that one is willing and open to change regarding one's thinking, feeling and behaviour.

Of course, "separating oneself out from the matrix of others"[38], especially from our beloved ones is never an easy task. This process

---

[38] Jordan, Judith V., Alexandra G. Kaplan, Jean B. Miller, Irene P. Stiver, and Janet L. Surrey.1991. *Women's Growth in Connection: Writings from the Stone Center.* NY: Guilford Press, p. 11.

is achieved through a sequence of painful experiences or crisis as the individual tries to claim independence and autonomy from others. But the result is an attainment of inner feeling of a separated individuation. There is always pain and difficulty It is worthy of note that one marks the difficulty associated with this process. Though it is not a pleasant experience, it exposes the self to the utilisation of the already acquired abilities and potentialities that have remained latent.

INTEGRATING THE COGNITIVE AND AFFECTIVE DOMAIN OF THE SELF

The human person does not possess dual nature: one rational and the other emotional. The human person is a unitary being who is open towards self-transcendence. The ego is holistic and functions as a 'whole'. Therefore, the self as a unified being grows and matures following the principle of totality. A situation whereby an aspect of the self dominates in a very pronounced manner retards the integrating process as a *whole* being. The unity in question here does not exclude the presence of conflicts and other internal divisions of the ego.

Cognition is not opposed to emotion as some philosophers hold (Plato). Nor does feeling inhibit the proper functioning of the cognitive domain, the rational thinking. There is always a healthy interaction between cognition and emotion. Both are inextricably linked[39]. Reason and passion are not enemies. Often, the content of one's emotions, flow from one's rational capacity. The emotions are only the result and consequence of an already thought phenomenon. As man's tool of survival, reason has two basic functions: cognition and evaluation. The process of cognition consists of discovering what things *are*, of identifying their nature, their attributes, and properties. The process of evaluation consists of man discovering the relationship of things to himself, of determining what is beneficial to

---

[39] Davidson, Richard J., Klaus R. Scherer, and Hill H. Goldsmith. 2003. *The Handbook of Affective Sciences*. NY: Oxford University Press, p. 572.

him and what is harmful, what he should seek and what to avoid. Despite our formidable intellectual abilities and successes, we need emotion to balance it.

A balanced self or fuller development of the person will be obtained by an integration of these domains in a complementary manner. None should dominate in an exaggerated way. When emotion overshadows cognition, it disrupts the rate of concentration. The working memory becomes low, that is "the ability to hold in mind all information relevant to the task at hand"[40]. There should be interdependence here. None should prevail over the other. One's emotional state may be unbalanced and immature. Although the cognitive transition is an imperative, it is worthy of note that spirituality is not synonymous with emotional blindness.

For this reason, the interdependent self is proposed to priests and religious. That is, a self that "is connected, fluid, flexible and participates in social relationships that guide action. A self that is oriented to the collective, meets obligations and conforms to norms. A self that defines life by contributing to the collective, is responsible with others for joint behaviour, is cooperative and subsumes self in the collective"[41]. After all, every human person is always in the state of becoming. In the different phases of becoming there comes growth since every experience is an opportunity for the self to grow. That is why the self cannot be understood or interpreted in form of a "monolithic unity" which is obtained once and for all. Rather the true self should be acquired in an ongoing process of integration, which connects cognitive, affective, and operational or active aspects with each other[42]. The self is *'not given'*, it requires a process of interaction for its proper maturity.

---

[40] Goleman, Daniel. 2005. *Emotional Intelligence. The 10th Anniversary Edition*. NY: Bantam Dell, p. 79.

[41] Hogg, Michael A., and Graham M. Vaughan. 2011, p. 619.

[42] Manenti, Alessandro., Stefano Guarinelli, and Hans Zollner. 2007. *Formation and the Person: Essays on Theory and Practice*. Leuven, Belgium: Peeters Press, 54.

One can rewrite his or her story, beginning with the '*inner child*', attending to it. For it is a coherent self which balances itself between the inner and outer changes that can relate positively with people. For when we plant a seed, its growth does not only depend on the external features like weather, type of soil, fertilizer etc., but also on the viability and healthiness of the seed planted. The self is in the process and not necessarily seen as moved by instincts and from the urges of the id, (if we take the self in the sense of ego in Freudian sense), but as a self-moving towards self-transcendence.

Conclusively, the human person is a psychological being with all the psychological needs there in. Man is not purely a spiritual being. Therefore, beside the spiritual longing (rational) and yearning for the mystical union with Christ, there is also that carnal desires (emotional) to gratify the psychological needs (sex, aggression, domination etc.). It is important that priests and religious are aware of this. The problem is not the co-existence of these longings and desires, but on the one that dominates. It is a difficult task to always allow the spiritual realm to dominate the Self, but it is also not impossible to do that.

RECLAIMING THE REPRESSED SELF: THE SHADOW

Carl Jung described the shadow as "the part of our personality that we repress because it conflicts with the way we wish to see ourselves"[43]. Some aspects of our lives do not correspond with our ideal self, that is, the person we aspire and think we should be (for example, desires, sexuality, aggression, exhibition etc.). They are rejected part of the self because they are below the standard of one's expectations of life. The shadow is the abandoned and neglected aspect of our personality which seeks every opportunity to survive. It carries along with it some principles and rules of life, which in most cases are parallel to the values and attitudes of one's life. It is

---

[43] Au, Wilkie., and Noreen Cannon. 1995. *Urgings of The Heart. A Spirituality of Integration*. NY: Paulist Press, p. 25.

the hidden self, exactly the opposite of one's conscious personality. The journey towards wholeness necessitates getting to know one's shadow and confronting its dynamics.

The shadow is formed early in life starting from the moral developmental stage. Beginning from the age of two, the child begins to observe and assimilate certain values from the parents and care-givers. For example, a child gradually learns that he or she is expected to co-exist with the other siblings, play with them, share toys with them, greet the elders etc. Gradually, the child grows in morality and acquires a sense of good and bad from the parents and care-givers. Sometimes this is achieved through cautioning, constant warning and in some cases through punishment. Parents use both power-assertion (physical punishment, beating) and non-power assertion (withdrawal of affect) method to enforce discipline. Hence, a boy who receives punishment for not greeting his or her elders learns by force that greeting is both a moral and social value. Nevertheless, growing up, it becomes clear to him that there are some people that he would not willingly like to greet, but still he must greet them to avoid punishment or to be acceptable by a group. In this way, repression sets in. The child learns to shape his or her behavior to suit the one that is acceptable by the family, society or any group. This is the gradual process of forming the shadow.

Reclaiming is a continuous process. Our shadow will always be present no matter the effort to annihilate it. When the shadow is brought to consciousness, the great energy therein becomes a source of motivation in reclaiming the real self. Nevertheless, in reclaiming the self, the objective is to include the shadow and accept it as part of our identity. For "we are enriched by the shadow; it makes us interesting, gives us depth and character, and strengthens our sense of identity. The more we know ourselves, the less fearful and defensive we need be"[44]. The good thing is to observe and recognize it. The human person is neither pure light or free of darkness; neither totally good nor totally bad. To accept this is unhealthy. Repression makes

---

[44] Au, Wilkie., and Noreen Cannon. 1995, p. 41.

it even worse, as well as its denial. The shadow can influence people so much and interfere with meaningful relationships, leading to its break-ups.

The shadow is observed in different ways in our everyday lives. Recognizing, accepting and integrating them when they are present is a major aid to gaining self-knowledge. There are different ways of recognizing our shadows. Through projection one can recognize one's shadows. Projection is the "perceiving and reacting to unacceptable inner impulses and their derivatives as though they were outside the self"[45]. Anytime we exhibit an intense judgment, or criticism about another person's behavior, it points towards our own shadow. For example, being too rigid and judgmental about those with sexual misconduct could be pointing to lack of sexual integration. One who has integrated his or her shadow will be humbler, *there go I if not for God's grace*, knowing that he or she is also capable of such unacceptable behavior. However, everything is not projection. Sometimes people will be reacting to an objective and outstanding moral evil – far from criticism. The difference is that whenever it is the case of projection, the emotion involved is intense involving even some physiological changes. It involves an exaggerated and excessive reaction towards the subject or the issue at hand.

Again, some slip of tongues (parapraxis) could be as a result of some repressed thoughts and feelings struggling to come into consciousness and recognition. Certain mistakes in speeches like mispronunciations and misplacement of some concepts are not mere mistakes, they are internal conflicts which carry important messages about oneself when processed. According to Freud, through them one can identify one's shadows.

Also, one can discover one's shadow by exploring the contents and process of one's humor. Not only that a good sense of humor helps to reduce tensions and makes the communication of difficult

[45] Gabbard, Glen O. 2005. *Psychodynamic Psychiatry in Clinical Practice.* Fourth Edition. American Psychiatric Publishing, Washington DC, p. 37.

messages easier, but it is a notable place where shadow resides in a hidden manner. It gives much information about what is stored up in the unconscious and the shadow.

Integrating the shadow helps us to attain wholeness and holiness. We do this by trying to be conscious. We cannot integrate the shadow whole and entire. At the same time, we are not to be disturbed or worried about the shadow since we are rather enriched by their presence.

Chapter Three
UNDERSTANDING AFFECTIVE MATURITY

AFFECTIVE MATURITY DOES NOT MEAN COLDNESS OR INDIFFERENCE

Affective maturity does not mean being cold or indifferent. It is not as if to say that priests and religious have lost anything affectively wise as to mourn which makes them perpetually cold and indifferent to being affectionate. They rather have it all: a free heart that loves all and therefore have every reason to be warm, passionate and affectionate in their relationships with all, irrespective of age, race, religion and gender. A state of apathy or trying to be emotionless is not helpful. In fact, Cencini believes that "the unemotional, empty-hearted celibate also runs the risk to confuse self-giving to God with a false interior peace and tranquility opposite to a dynamic offering, or to reduce one's consecration to a dead fulfilment of everything, including one's vitality"[46]. The point is not denying one's feelings but rather of expressing them in a mature manner. Chesterton maintains that the lion being together with the lamb is not expected to become like the lamb as that would be unfair and brutality to the nature and essence of the lion. But, that the real problem and question is whether the lion can lie down with the lamb and still retain his royal ferocity[47]. This is a challenge, it is not all about avoiding the opposite sex or the same sex but being and relating with them in a mature and responsible manner, without losing the essence of religious life in purity and chastity. It is about balancing emotion with reason. This will require the use of coping mechanisms like sublimation, altruism and delaying gratification. Something essential would be missing in the sister's

---

[46] Cencini, Amaedo R. 2009. *Virginity and Celibacy Today*. Nairobi, Kenya: Paulines Publications, p.51.

[47] Chesterton, G.K 1990. *Orthodoxy*. New York, page 98.

52

apostolate and priestly ministry, if they are no longer warm with people they work for and work with.

> *It is in that convergence of spiritual people becoming active and active people becoming spiritual that the hope of humanity now rests.*
>
> VAN JONES

In the same vein, spirituality is not synonymous with being cold or indifferent. Maturity does not consist in not being expressive. Being cold or indifferent can also affect one's spiritual development and interpersonal functioning. For according to Van Jones, "it is in that convergence of spiritual people becoming active and active people becoming spiritual that the hope of humanity now"[48]. It is active priests and religious who attract souls to God through their words, gestures and i Parappully, Jose and Jose Kuttianmattathil. 2012. *Psychosexual Integration and Celibate Maturity. Handbook for Religious and Priestly Formation.* Bosco Society of Printing and Graphic Training, New Delhi, p.120. n fact good behaviors. Dull and passive priests and religious have less positive influence on people, especially on the youths. A spirituality which does not flow into activity through pastoral ministry is dormant and not harnessed.

Furthermore, the psychologist Umoren coined an antithesis of affective maturity, as "the inability to be in touch with oneself, or knowing one's passion, needs, desires, impulses and reaction"[49]. In other words, awareness is vital to affective maturity and anyone who operates his or her life lacking in self-awareness lives a fragmentary life. Those with low self-esteem avoid self-knowledge due to their low capacity for anxiety tolerance. Awareness of their real emotions and passions add to their pains. Therefore, repressing their real self-

---

[48] Parappully, Jose and Jose Kuttianmattathil. 2012. *Psychosexual Integration and Celibate Maturity. Handbook for Religious and Priestly Formation.* Bosco Society of Printing and Graphic Training, New Delhi, p.120.

[49] Umoren, Linus. 2012. "Human Sexuality: Crisis and Challenges in Formation". Pp.55-86 in *The Catholic Voyage. A Publication of the Conference of Major Superiors of Nigeria*, Vol. 9.

knowledge masquerades as maturity and expresses itself in pseudo serenity and calmness. Hence, before others, people of this sort appear as mature people who are in control of their lives, while they do not know themselves. And so, what are they in control of?

CODEPENDENCY: AN ENEMY OF AFFECTIVE MATURITY

The term 'codependency' was coined in the 1980s to describe the emotionally dependent relationship on another person who was dependent on a substance. Typically, codependency was seen in a partner or child of an alcoholic or addict. In this relationship, the substance abuser is wrapped up in their addiction while the codependent person, not being on any mind-altering substance, feels emotionally dependent on the alcoholic/addict. This person could be mentally ill, have a personality disorder, or be emotionally or physically abusive. Though the codependent person may not be addicted to alcohol or other drugs, his or her traits and behaviors can be just as self-destructive as those of the addicted person[50]. It is an illness which is as a result of loss of authentic selfhood. In this case the person operates with a false self, a self that has been made over to the ego and the service of other people. The real/true self is repressed.

In the article, *Co-dependency, An Emerging Issue*, Robert Subby described codependency as an emotional, psychological, and behavioral condition that develops as a result of an individual's prolonged exposure to, and practice of a set of oppressive rules---rules which prevent the open expression of feeling as well as the direct discussion of personal and interpersonal problems. It involves a pattern of cognition and emotion which is destructive to the human person. Codependents lack a sense of autonomy and direction in their lives. Consequently, they are like 'slaves of others', as they let other people direct and rule their lives. They depend excessively on other people for many things.

---

[50] Bailey, Jeanette P. 2010, *Emotional Freedom Techniques for Codependency Recovery*, Self-Publishing.com, p. 18.

The psycho-genesis of this maladaptive behavior of codependency is traced back to dysfunctional families where neglects, different types of abuses and severe application of rules were daily norms. Children who grew up in this type of family suffer a lot and are 'without centers' because they are compelled by circumstance to develop a weak ego and disorganized ego structure. They grew up with conditional love from their parents and care-givers. Consequently, as adults, the *inner child* which was terribly wounded; never loved and appreciated; and abused seek these compensations in different ways. One of the pronounced ways of doing this is by compulsive rendering help to others through which they boost their self-worth. Because their sense of inner security comes from the outside, it matters to them that people affirm and praise them. Their main identity and strength to operate in daily life comes from people's positive evaluation. And so, the quest for this compels them to constant activity and 'doing for others'. This is an escape from confronting their true self. With this they are not to be in touch with their chronic emptiness.

At the level of affect control, they have an unconscious and excessive need to bond with people. This need ignites in them the urge to consistently seek for opportunities to do that. This inner drive leaves them even insensitive to people's feelings, so that they fail to understand that a person is not emotionally available and ready for their friendship. Given their blindness to this reality, they spend their time and energy nurturing a relationship where they remain perpetual objects and servers. Still, codependents feel normal and keep struggling to keep the relationship. They are incapacitated to withdraw given the fact that they were raised in dysfunctionality. As a result, what ordinarily is dysfunction appears normal to them.

Codependents are experts in repressing their thoughts and feelings due to fear of not being accepted. They have the tendency of hiding their real emotions and putting on the acceptable ones. This makes them habitual white lie tellers because they always operate with the false self. Their ideal self is never in agreement with their actual self. There is a pronounced discrepancy between the two which the codependent is aware but tries to put it off, notwithstanding the pains.

Again, codependents are need inventors and initiators. They create needs for others and exhibit a high sense of responsibility to take care of people's needs. They have an exaggerated sense of care for others. In their compulsive nature of putting the needs of others before their own, they neglect their primary needs and self-care. Their satisfaction lies in satisfying people's needs. They are chronic pleasers and lack the capacity to say 'no'. In doing this, they are always busy and mainly workaholics. This is a defence mechanism to avoid confronting their true sense of chronic emptiness. With their perception that they are not *good enough*, they break their necks in search of activities to prove their worth.

Codependents misinterpret the scriptures to justify their behaviours. They interpret the spirituality of asceticism, mortification and self-sacrifice in a distorted manner. This is where we see the unconscious inconsistency in action. So that a priest who is a codependent may spend his time in caring for others. Before others, it is a Christian virtue and ideal. But, it is simply a subtle way of satisfying the ego. They run the risk of suffering from stress, depression and burnout. In this case, the dissonant need of affective dependence is the motivational force, the manifest attribute is affiliation, love, empathy, generosity and availability. It is for this that people address codependents as nice and holy people, without knowing that their service and care for others is another way of getting fulfilment in an unconscious manner. Since service is at the core of their nature, every opportunity gearing towards that helps to reinforce that need of acceptance and recognition. In other words, their service is contaminated. It is not coming from the gospel value. Part of the problem is also due to the way some spiritual masters distort the spirituality of self-sacrifice or love as neglecting one's self-care for the good of others. These masters tend to associate selfishness with those who are assertive or those who believe in caring for themselves first and then others. They fail to harmonize caring for others and caring for oneself.

Codependents are far from affective maturity. Confronting the root cause of codependency and examining their influence in one's private life and in the ministry liberates one more for total self-giving in the work assigned to him or her. Giving up the opportunity given to others to exercise undue control over us in order to please them and giving up the desire to control others in order to feel secure are the greatest task of a codependent. Neither excessive self-concern nor a marked neglect of self-care is recommended. One must attend to his or her legitimate needs.

WHAT THEN IS AFFECTIVE MATURITY?

Affective maturity centers primarily on acquiring the relational skills to genuinely and adaptively observe, identify and to express one's true feelings with oneself, in the presence of the other and the Other, within one's unique life experiences. Growth in affective maturity embraces also admitting and embracing old hurts inflicted either to people or on oneself, and the negative scripts and paradigms from one's past life, and the conscious decision to forgive and to carry on in life with integrity. Progress in this area requires patience with oneself, others, God and the environment, while honesty is an important virtue in this sphere. The principal notion of affective maturity is not merely the renunciation of sex, or repression of the urge for an affair. After all, celibacy or virginity does not consist only in not having sex, or not marrying, or living alone, or in keeping rules and regulations, and in fact avoiding transgression of some moral norms. It is rather the conscious and deliberate decision not to exclude anyone from the network of relationship or from the bond of fraternal charity. So that love is not based on emotional attraction or secondary gain. Exclusivity, bonding, tie, are meant for marriages and not for the consecrated virgin or the celibate. The priest or religious is not a passive introvert, neither is he or she an extrovert who lacks prudence in his or her dealings with others. Granted that the strong passions of the heart gradually disappear or become weak with age, it is also possible that for some it increases with age. Self-knowledge and awareness help one to realize and be at home with one's rhythm of life.

The substance of affective maturity is genuine love. To be affectively mature means having a heart free from all forms of attachment. Affective freedom liberates one and renders him or her free to love all creatures, to love God. It also creates the room for not excluding anybody or binding anyone exclusively to oneself, not to be selective as is obtainable in the logic of human love. In other words, love is the substance. When one attains maturity affectively, one "chooses not to exclude anyone. One gives up the criteria of human benevolence and sympathy, which includes some and excludes others purely on the grounds of spontaneous attraction and personal interest rather than the interest of the other"[51]. In this case, one no longer sees a friend as an object who is 'important-for-me', but one relates with a friend who is 'important-in-him/herself' as a valuable creature made in the image and likeness of God. One respects the other for the intrinsic value of that person, and respects also the other person's philosophy of life.

One who is affectively mature has the capacity to control one's impulses. This means that the individual, while being free and spontaneous, controls reasonably his or her emotions and impulses. Therefore, question of los-

> When one attains maturity affectively, one chooses not to exclude anyone. One gives up the criteria of human benevolence and sympathy, which includes some and excludes others purely on the grounds of spontaneous attraction and personal interest rather than the interest of the other.
>
> AMAEDO CENCINI

ing one's temper does not arise. Rather one integrates one's emotions. The question of falling in love does not arise also. Rather one grows in love. He or she is not carried away by the waves of passions, sentiments or desires. The person is objective in his or her choices and decisions. People of these calibers have the capacity to delay gratification of any sort and put the body under control. Lack

---

[51] Cencini, Amaedo R. 2009, p. 15.

of the capacity for impulse control is a clear sign of one who is affectively immature. Therefore, "immaturity is seen when a person acts out impulsively without adequate control of emotions or when a person is rigid and over-controlled thereby losing spontaneity and enjoyment"[52].

The ability to grow in affective maturity is rooted in the effects of nature and nurture, especially the type of affectional bond which an infant had from birth. Self-awareness, self-consciousness, and the ability to be at home with one's emotions, appreciation of one's gift and acceptance of one's limitations, all are prerequisites for affective maturity. The parameter of time becomes important where the individual tries to bring his or her past emotional experiences in harmony with the present, and this helps him or her to prepare and aspire for a more flourishing future life. Maturity consists in integrating the past with the present. Therefore, every attitude which leads one to live in the present without past or future, which encloses one in a past refusing every element of novelty, or which induces one to live dreaming of a future detached from the present which carries an entire past with it, all such attitudes characterize one who has remained psychologically immature, and specifically deficient in affective maturity[53]. It makes one odd in relationships.

THE PRINCIPLES OF AFFECTIVE MATURITY

For apostolic effectiveness of priests and religious, there is need for growth in affective maturity. Apart from acquiring the necessary relational skills to express one's feelings, maturity also consists in understanding the diversity and individual differences and developing the capacity for dialogue. The aspects of affective maturity which this book will consider are emotional regulation, self-regulation, psychosocial stability, psychosexual integration, healthy relationship, healthy self-esteem and responsible use of freedom.

---

[52] Cencini, Amaedo R. 2009, p. 30.
[53] Imoda, Franco. 2007, p. 112.

a. Emotional Regulation

The result of poor management of affect and emotion is unhappiness. Some priests and religious fall prey to this. For the fact that emotions are '*given*', one may not have the whole control over them, but one can control what one is emotional. One can make some adjustments and changes in what triggers the emotion and how one responds to that. Again, it is good to mention that emotions are contagious, so that people can dump their negative feelings on others, and this can elicit the same distressing emotions. There are also some neurological and physical consequences of such response. One must learn the best process of emotional regulation.

Individuals are to ascertain their level of emotional development. This gives information on how an individual experience, assimilates and interprets his or her feelings and emotions beginning from infancy to adulthood. The greatest aid here is personal consciousness examen, and daily journaling when a priest or a sister willingly articulates his or her experiences. Psychotherapy is also of great importance. With this consciousness, one can avoid emotional wanting which is linked to the here and now. Instead, one is to adopt rational wanting, that is, "a reflective evaluation based on beneficial to me /not beneficial to me. An evaluation that goes beyond the immediate and sensitive interest for the object because it reverts to the values and aims that the subject had proposed to him/herself"[54]. It is good to delay the gratification which one gets from emotional acts. This is helpful, though the person may experience the pain, but gradually it becomes part of the person. For instance, a sister who is used to emotionally responding back to every unpleasant statement made in the group, taking it personally and therefore quarrelling about it, must be ready to 'let go' of the fulfilment she gets from quarrelling and take herself less serious and less important.

---

[54] Cencini, Amaedo, and Alessandro Manenti. 2010, p. 69.

b. Self-Regulation

Emotional regulation precedes self-regulation. When one is emotionally regulated, he or she puts less energy in trying to regulate the self in its entirety. Regulation is the process through which a system or a psychological functioning domain harmonizes the level of another to maintain an adaptive balance or equilibrium in response to internal or external stimulation. Self-regulation refers to the "automatic response of healthy individuals to salient discrepancies between expectation and reality as they perceive it. They may involve cognition or behaviour, and almost always are attended by affect"[55]. The capacity to regulate the self is the foundation of healthy psychological functioning. This gives people a sense of stability in their major areas of life and the capacity to control their impulses. For this they use mature coping mechanisms to keep their interpersonal relationships positive. This also allows them to perceive others in an objective manner and to believe that others perceive them in a realistic manner. Those who lack self-regulation are prone to all forms of acting outs and psychopathology.

Priests and religious are to be encouraged to be conscientious in all their dealings. When they develop a high sense of conscientiousness which helps them in acquiring the virtues of confidence, discipline, orderliness, and even the strength to integrate their painful experiences, they can regulate themselves properly. Hence, they are confident in their capacity to elaborate and process their experiences, and therefore control their behaviour.

In fact, the yardstick for a self which is regulated lies in one's capacity to be consistent in living a positive life. Consistency here means that one's needs are syntonic with one's values. This can happen either at the conscious or unconscious level of being. It implies that an individual has repeatedly practiced a virtue to the point that it has become part and parcel of the person. The different domains of growth and development are harmonized in this process. For example, an individual who is consistent in helping others automatically

---

[55] Hoyle, Rick H. 2010, p. 1.

integrates this virtue, so that even when the cognitive domain wants to disintegrate (must I be the only one helping out, let others do), the affective domain disagrees (the heart beats restlessly and desires to help out), and the conative domain approves of it (gets into action, and off he or she goes). In this sense, the self is regulated and is integrated.

However, self-regulation requires effortful control, that is, "ability to inhibit a dominant response to perform a subdominant response, to detect errors, and to engage in planning"[56]. It requires an inner strength which can go beyond the physical weakness, looking beyond the secondary gain and the present moment. In fact, it involves the capacity to maintain a flexible ego, and to adapt it adequately according to situations. It also maintains other functions of the ego like processing information, planning and modulating emotions. Those with internal locus of control achieve this easily.

c. Psycho-social Stability

A major aspect of affective maturity is the capacity to experience others in relationship, to build and sustain healthy friendships. Psychosocial stability is about being free and open-minded in loving others and in letting oneself be loved. Wittberg lucidly asserts that "a solitary Christian is a contradiction"[57]. If this is so, it becomes even more contradiction when those who are called to apostolic ministry live solitary lives. Neither total individualism which is a form of narcissistic tendency and selfishness, nor total dependence on people which is suffocating is recommended. Psychosocial stability gives the balance.

Apart from a close and intimate relationship with Christ which priests and religious must make effort to develop and sustain, a warm and affectionate relationship with one another is imperative for their ministry. The important thing in a social relationship is not the quantity of social interaction with friends, but the depth, the quality, the

---

56 Rothbart, Mary K., and Rosario M. Rueda. 2005. p, 169.

57 Wittberg, Patricia S. 2012. *Building Strong Church Communities: A Sociological Overview*. Mahwah, NJ: Paulist Press p. 27.

level of intimacy and the joy derived from the relationship. Good quality interaction which includes genuineness, sincerity, truthfulness and transparency is required. Psychosocial stability presupposes warmth in relationships. The author Wittberg highlights the aspect of community as a place for social connectivity and asserting of one's identity. She recapitulates that solitary life is hostile and incompatible with the nature of man. According to her, no individual can sustain the pains of loneliness without breaking down both physically and emotionally. This is because right from the cradle, there is a connectivity between the mother, the caregiver, and the outside world. This produces a deep relationship which is rooted in the social structure of man, without which it becomes difficult for man to have a solid identity and self-concept. Simply put, "for us to be, we must be in relation to others"[58].

Psycho-social maturity helps priests and religious to learn how to be with others and be happy, without being either withdrawn from the group or overshadowing the group.

> *Is there someone with whom we can really be ourselves, share our private thoughts and feelings without fear or pretence? This is what intimacy is all about.*
>
> PARAPPULLY JOSE

One who is psychosocially stable can enjoy intimacy. In this context, intimacy refers simply to that capacity of a person to freely and joyfully experience another person more closely both physically, emotionally and spiritually[59]. There is a kind of affinity which goes beyond family ties and bonds. Normally, this involves sacrificing and investing energy for the well-being of the other. In intimacy there is two people. One who is psychosocially integrated can enjoy it without transgressing or compromising one's values and moral principles. In fact, genuine and authentic intimacy is a characteristic of a mature adult and leads to happiness. The degree to

---

[58] Wittberg, Patricia S. 2012 p. 1.

[59] Parappully, Jose and Jose Kuttianmattathil. 2012, p. 99.

which one can cooperate or be interdependent in a relationship is one of the signs of psychological maturity. In this, most battle with autonomy and independence. Attainment of psychosocial maturity means that one no longer supresses the longing for genuine or authentic intimacy with the other, but is open to it, accepts it and experiences it in a healthy and meaningful manner. Not having friends with which to share one's innermost feelings and secret experiences contribute greatly to depression of some priests and religious.

Intimacy in this context which has nothing to do with physical nakedness or any related construct, but "psychological nakedness" where those involved are not only comfortable to talk about their successes, joys, virtues, ambitions, desires, longings, but also share their failures, pains and fantasies. To this the psychologist Parappully asks, "Is there someone with whom we can really be ourselves, share our private thoughts and feelings without fear or pretence? This is what intimacy is all about"[60]. According to him, it is all about cultivation of trust and transparency in close relationships. Priests and religious try to avoid this natural need. They resort to workaholism which eventually lands them to burnout. They also avoid this by relating to people only at professional level without paying attention to their personal needs.

d. Psychosexual Integration

Sexuality is a gift from God. The book of Genesis presents the goodness of sexuality to us. For God said, "Let us make man in our image, after our likeness..." (Cfr. Gn. 1: 26- 28). God is good and cannot but reproduce goodness in his creation. Everything God made was good, including human beings (Cfr. Gen. 1:31). Sexuality is both a gift and a mystery since it highlights the fact that man is made in the likeness of God. Sexuality is of divine origin, good, blessed and given to man. The fact of God creating male and female points to gender difference. Everything about man is good; sexual organs and sexual acts. In fact, Ferder and Heagle highlight the fact that "it is God

---

[60] Parappully, Jose and Jose Kuttianmattathil. 2012, p. 101.

who 'thought up' pelvic pleasure, organism, and sexual passion and placed a capacity for these experiences into our bodies, into our 'inmost selves', from the very beginning"[61]. The whole part of our body is holy. Therefore, sexual feelings, arousals, longings and images are freely generated in the mind as a process of expression of this gift of sexuality. These act as spontaneous expressions and processes toward sexual and human fulfilment as sexual beings. Sexual feelings and desires are good in themselves and are ethically and morally neutral. It is one's decision to carry out a behaviour, consciously and deliberately that gives the action a moral worth and meaning.

The limitations of human beings (including the celibates) is expressed in their unconscious search to be completed by another. This can only be possible by couples who are into marriage. And this intrinsic need does not in any way respect anybody or any status. The temptation is to indulge in the reduction of sexuality to exclusively an attraction for the opposite sex. This negative view is a block to grasping the richness of sexuality especially in the energy that goes with it. False spiritualism about sex which does not allow one to grasp the true meaning of sexuality is a hinderance to psychological maturity and psychosexual stability. Flesh and spirit are not two opposing forces as observed by the Gnostics who believe that the spirit is opposed to the flesh. Instead, we get great energy from sexuality which "opens the way to relation and reciprocity, towards love and mutual self-giving"[62]. On the other hand, renunciation of sexual intimacy is not an obstacle to healthy living and psychological balance. Human

---

[61] Ferder, F. and J. Heagle. 1997. *Your Sexual Self: Pathway to Authentic Intimacy*. Mumbai: St Pauls, p. 61.

[62] Man is called to love and to self-giving in unity of body and spirit. Femininity and masculinity are complementary gifts. Human sexuality is therefore an integral part of the capacity for love that God has inscribed in man and woman [...] The human body, male or female, seen in the mystery of creation, is not only source of fruitfulness and protection, as in the whole of the natural order, but it is also encloses, from 'the beginning' the 'espousal' attribute, i.e. the capacity to express that love by which the person becomes a gift. Through this gift he actualizes the very sense of his being and existence. Cf. John Paul II, General Audience, 16 January 1980.

sexuality is relation oriented, opening of oneself to others despite the sacrifices it entails. It is a responsible and courageous refusal to give in to the syndrome of isolation and withdrawal from others.

Sexuality is generative. It means that one is open to give life to others as he or she has received life from God. It becomes fruitful in many ways, appreciating the differences there are in people, apostolic initiative, etc. It is simply life and all-round expressions of life.

Another vital aspect of affective maturity is sexual integration. It is one of the most difficult challenges of priests and religious today. This is more so in the contemporary society which is sexually permissive, and where love is almost synonymous with sex. No one can escape this challenge, whether by denying its existence or by spiritualizing it. Efforts to exercise one's ministry effectively must include sexuality in all its ramifications. Any journey towards integration must include the body, the embodied self in its relational aspects both with the Other and the other. As mentioned earlier, the body and spirit are not opposing to each other. Sensuality and sexuality must agree at a point. We cannot deny the goodness of our body, otherwise we reject God who chose to have a body like us.

The word 'psycho' originates from the Greek word *psyche*, meaning the human soul, mind or spirit. It therefore refers to all related constructs to the mental and emotional attributes of an individual. While the word 'sexual' originates from the Latin word *sexus*. It refers to "dividing rather than uniting" which is opposite of what we would ordinarily think. Psychologically speaking, sexual is related to sexuality and can be described as "the feelings and attitudes a person has about his or her body, sex role, and relationships"[63]. It is also the capacity for sexual feelings which is manifested through gaze, touch, words and actions.

Psycho-sexual integration entails a conscious effort to harmonize all the elements which constitute the cognitive, emotional and

---

[63] Meeks, Linda and Heit, Philip. 2001. *Sexuality and Character Education K-12*. Chicago, Every day learning Corporation, p. 730.

sexual aspects of one's life. It is a conscious and personal journey which one undertakes as an emotional being who is spirit incarnate. This journey is meaningful and fruitful only in one's relational life, with God, oneself, and others. Sexual integration also embraces the sexual energies, arousals, experiences and the decision to adapt *eros*[64] more maturely in one's life as one seeks unity with the Transcendent. When people combine these elements of their lives well, including the internal (biological, and hormonal influences regarding sexuality) and external (physical appearance, social and moral ethics regarding sexuality) potentials and functions adaptively, one can now be described as a sexual integrated person. Psychosexual integration is a process which lasts from birth to death. Beginning from the biological and hormonal dynamics which begins from the unification of the sperm and ovum, to the individuation of the chromosomes, to the development of the foetus, to the itching of this foetus to come out to the physical world, to the developmental processes from childhood to adulthood and to late adult, and then death. Each stage has its own challenges regarding sexuality. However, if this process is disrupted along the line, one's capacity for mature relationship will be affected.

Psychosexual integration means that there is a progressive combination of all the constituents of psychic, emotional and sexual aspects of one's life. When there is a harmony among these, and

---

[64] According to Rolheiser Ronald, *eros* was the mythical Greek god of love, and his name eventually began to be used in literature and Greek philosophy as rich word to connote the deepest pulse within life itself, encompassing all aspects of love: friendship, care, romance, emotional obsession, sexual attraction, pragmatic planning and arranging, and altruism and sacrifice. There is no word more apt than eros to describe the deepest energy and fire inside us, especially as this makes itself felt in our youth. The mythic god of love is inside us, with all his grandiosity, hungers, thirsts, and lusts. We feel this as a powerful pulse for life, as a buoyancy that trumps every death wish, as an irresistible greed for experience, as a relentless pressure within our sexuality, as a desire to taste things, to know all things, to be known by others, to be everywhere, and as a desire for heroism and martyrdom. Cf. Rolheiser Ronald 2014.

this harmony is manifested in a consistent behavioural pattern of an adult, a person is referred to as psychosexually integrated person. In this also, the dynamism of one's physical, moral, social, and even spiritual life in each context is not left behind. All these contribute to maturity.

It also entails understanding the real meaning and concept of celibate chastity and ways of sustaining it. The deliberate choice of priests and religious to remain celibates presupposes dealing with their sexuality both in the broad and narrow sense of it. This includes their bodies, their manhood/womanhood, and their ability to channel all their affection in purity to Christ. Chastity/celibacy here will simply mean "a moral virtue that regulates the exercise of sexuality according to the state of life of the person and the person's values, at the same time respecting the nature of sexuality itself"[65]. In the case of priests and religious, it calls for total abstinence from any genital pleasure, but not limited to that.

Furthermore, chastity "is not hard observance and dutiful continence, or an idea of perfection that saddens the one who undertakes it. Even less is it renunciation born out of depreciating the body or of fearing sex, which ends up impoverishing the false ascetic"[66]. Celibate chastity is not merely avoiding sex or any genital actions, but rather an education of the mind and body towards a true expression of love and sentiments in the footsteps of Christ. It is not simply a question of sisters or priests retaining their virginity in the biological sense of the word. It is also not enough to abstain from all forms of 'pleasures of the flesh'. More importance is to be given to "grasp in its luminosity and ambiguity, the indelible presence of the Spirit, the 'Paschal spark', and to favour the powerful drive that sexuality impresses on a fruitful relation"[67]. A chaste person is one who consistently harmonizes his or her feelings, thoughts and actions in the model of Christ. It means they are in consonant with the gospel values.

---

[65] Cencini, Amaedo R. 2009, p. 72.

[66] Cencini, Amaedo R. 2009, p. 73.

[67] Cencini, Amaedo R. 2009, p. 74.

Despite the happy self-donation in celibacy and virginity, priests and nuns are faced with the fiery force of sexuality. Therefore, they must not be naïve or underrate the power of sexual instincts. Clear relational boundaries are protective.

Despite the happy self-donation in celibacy and virginity, priests and nuns are faced with the fiery force of sexuality. Therefore, they must not be naïve or under-rate the power of sexual instincts. Clear relational boundaries are protective. This is to avoid channelling the energy of the *eros* in an unhealthy manner. Without psychosexual integration, celibate chastity will be fruitless. As such, celibate persons may tend to channel their sexual energies wrongly and in selfish ways. Psychosexual maturity demands that celibates accept themselves as sexual beings, who can also have genital arousals and sexual longings. These are intrinsic to male and female. It is enough that one engages into good relationships and expresses genuine love. Genital intimacy does not form part of psychosexual integration. It rather disintegrates the celibate who indulges in it. Genital intimacy is a desire and not a need. In the world of desires there are many possibilities which does not diminish the dignity of the human person when not fulfilled. But in the world of necessity, a need which is not fulfilled and attended to, diminishes the human person. For example, when the need of clothing or shelter is not fulfilled, it is an embarrassment to the human nature. But when the desire to purchase the best car is not fulfilled, it does not affect the essence of man. One can still go on public transport. Genuine love and relationship can still be simple, true, intense and deep without any genital intimacy.

Some argue that celibacy is against nature. Sometimes this argument unconsciously affects priests and religious who now feel they are missing something vital for their well-being. To this, the great psychiatrist Sipe, responded that a life without sex is as natural as anything that can be natural. Even in the animal kingdom, some species of animals spend their lives without mating. For example, some species of lions who feel more superior to others live and die without mating. They do this to conserve their energy and spend it for fighting and protecting other members of the species. Continuing, he maintains that sexual bonding and reproduction are the norm in nature, but not a universal or invariable norm. By nature, some males and females are not meant to bond or reproduce. This natural determination is a variant for the good of the group[68]. If animals can renounce sexual intimacy for the sake conserving energy for fighting, how much more the celibate who does that for the sake of a higher value. Hence, the celibate who freely, responsibly and generously decides to renounce sexual intimacy for the sake of the Kingdom of God should not in any way feel half complete. He or she loses nothing, but rather possesses more, the most valuable Treasure. To this, the renowned author Mannath insists that:

> The one who chooses celibacy is a normal woman or man. I do not stop being normal. I do not lose my sexual identity, with all that it implies: body, emotions, reactions, fantasies, attractions, ability to relate sexually, capacity to bear children and bring them up. I do not – and should not – lose my capacity for tenderness or intimacy or for deep caring, that I am capable of as a man or woman. It would be pathetic if, in the name of celibacy, we were to amputate our humanity, become less human, less caring, less tender-hearted, or less willing to give ourselves in love[69].

Again, it is important that individuals learn and understand their sexual orientations and their uniqueness in matters of sexuality. Individuals have unique sexual self. The sexual self is that aspect of who we are through which we express our sexuality. This self encompasses the belief and value system, attitudes and even images and symbols which link up the body and mind in the realm of sexual-

---

[68] Sipe, Richard, A. W. 1996. *Celibacy: A way of loving, Living and Serving.* Liguori, MO: Truimph Books, p. 35-36.

[69] Parappully, Jose and Jose Kuttianmattathil, p. 503.

ity[70]. Sexuality here entails more than biological attributes of male or female. It goes beyond the mere sexual affair. The more important aspect of this is intimate relational issues, family and society at large. Each man or woman has in potency the capacity of creating and experiencing his or her sexuality both positively and negatively. The foundations for healthy and fulfilling expressions of sexuality in adulthood are internalized during the early stages of life. Nevertheless, biological processes help to shape and mould the sexual self. Childhood sexual curiosity, explorations and self-stimulation for pleasure are natural ways of experiencing the sexual self even at that early stage. These experiences are typical for a growing child, although adult reactions and cautions towards this attitude help the self to stabilise in a healthy way. Some cultural, moral, and social prohibitions accompany these as well and have influence on the developing sexual ego. The hormonal shifts from childhood, to young adult, to mid-life experiences affect the entire sexual-self.

The sexual self is not static. It changes with age, experience, and biological maturation. In fact, it is a lifelong *work-in-progress* in the unconscious state. It is this sexual self that craves for love and intimate relationship with the opposite sex. As the Self-matures in age, the psychological need for affective dependence increases and attraction increases. The psychic energy instils in the person the great desire for a unification of the sex difference. The desire to complement and be complemented sexually increases. Fantasies of even an unhealthy affair are sometimes nurtured in one's heart and mind. Longings for dates with intimate friends in other to enjoy pleasurable affective mood occupy meaningful moments of one's experience. These are natural experiences of a normal person. It is important to be conscious of the age factor which contributes more to emotional and sexual vulnerability. As one matures in life, one's orgasmic responsiveness increases, sexual attraction, and arousal become an existential challenge. However, with spiritual and psy-

---

[70] Ellison, Carol R. 2000. *Women's Sexualities. Generations of Women Share Intimate Secrets of Sexual Self-Acceptance.* Oakland, CA: New Harbinger Publications, p.13.

chological aids, one can integrate one's sexuality. The solution is not repression of these urges which comes up in future life in more sexually distorted forms. It implies accepting the inner workings of the bodily chemistry: arousal, attraction, fantasies, day-dreams, and sexual desires, naming and accepting them. This is a process and never achieved once and for all.

More important is the understanding of how one's whole sexuality fits into one's unique and dynamic self. It is this understanding that helps in psychosexual integration. Hence, the way a priest or a sister will express his or her sexuality becomes totally different from the way a married man would do. This saves one from certain embarrassments. This understanding helps to maintain one's peace of mind and prevents one from some self-destructive behaviours which may constitute pain and block towards personal integration. So that with the emotion of love, for example, the strong pull to have an affair with a loved one is transformed into experiencing a healthy and warm relationship.

SIGNS OF AFFECTIVE IMMATURITY

Some attitudes and dispositions do not favour psychosexual integration. They are: homosexuality, masturbation, affective dependency, addictions, aggression and other forms. Granted the Lord has not called only those who are psychosexually integrated to priestly and religious life, they are to make effort to avoid attitudes which may hinder the process of integration.

a. Homosexuality

Lack of sexual integration and identity give rise to homosexuality. According to Coleman, a homosexual is one who has "a predominant, persistent and exclusive psychosexual attraction toward members of the same sex. A homosexual person is one who feels sexual desire for and a sexual responsiveness to persons of the same sex and who seeks or should like to seek actual fulfilment of this desire by sexual acts with a person of the same sex"[71]. It is good to mention immediately that a homosexual is not a gay. A gay is one who has admitted his or her sexual orientation as a homosexual as an integral part of his or her personality. He or she is at home with this fact and communicates it freely to others. They are at ease with being referred to homosexuals. According to the Catechism of the Catholic Church, homosexual acts are contrary to the natural law. They close the sexual act to the gift of life. They do not proceed from a genuine affective and sexual complementarity. Under no circumstances can they be approved (*CCC*: 2357). The Church calls them to chastity.

Psychologists have many theories about the origin of homosexuality. Some believe it is a genetic factor, some attribute it to abnormal prenatal or postnatal hormonal imbalance. However, most believe that homosexuality is a combination of biological, sociocultural, psychodynamic and situational factors. For the psychoanalytic, homosexuality has its origin in distorted parent-child relationships, lack of close bonding and secure attachment. According to the psychologist Cencini, it is caused by failure to identify with the parent of the same sex in early stages of growth. In this case, structural homosexuality becomes the case. It can also be non-structural as in the case of being caused by some experiences that distorted or blocked the normal development from the homo-erotic to the hetero-erotic phase in pre-adolescence[72]. This makes homosexuality a complicated issue. Although the *Diagnostic and Statistical Manual of Mental Disorders* (DSM-III) eliminated homosexuality as an illness in 1987, the clear thing is that it causes distress today both in the Church and in the society at present. It therefore becomes very important that people be sincere in evaluating the influence this can have in their relationship with God, others and their ministry. When homosexuality constitutes a pronounced block to this, the one in-

---

[71] Coleman, G.D. 199. *Human sexuality: An all-embracing Gift*. NY: Alba House, p. 211.

[72] Cencini, Amaedo R. 2009, p. 47.

volved is advised to seek help. Any ideology that does not promote this is against human flourishing.

Worthy of note is the fact that homosexuality does not only consist in same-sex attraction. It consists mainly in their great difficulty in relationships. They are self-absorbent and have difficulty allowing people into their lives in an unconditional manner. They are objectively deficient in their interpersonal relations. Since relationship with other people is essential for psychological growth, they grow to become psychologically immature. In their world, there is denial of the Other and the other and a pronounced self-centeredness.

b. Masturbation

Masturbation entails a sexual stimulation of a person's genitals to the extent of sexual gratification. It is one of the manifestations of neurosis in a technical sense. It has some physical and biological consequences. It is a block to spiritual progress. Masturbation becomes abnormal when there is a marked attachment to it as a means of release of sexual tensions and sexual gratification. It is a form of self-absorption which is characteristic of narcissism. The Church has always maintained that masturbation is morally bad and disordered action (*CCC*, 2352), The deliberate use of the sexual faculty, for whatever reason, outside of marriage, is essentially contrary to its purpose. In masturbation, sexual pleasure is sought outside the sexual relationship which is demanded by the moral order and in which the total meaning of mutual self-giving and human procreation in the context of true love is achieved. Lack of personal maturity depends on this.

The psychogenesis of masturbation varies from one person to the other. For some it is simply to release tension or to get rid of some present frustrations. Some engage in it as a result of insomnia (sleep disorder), or lack of capacity to manage their solitude. In fact, for most people it serves as a coping mechanism. Some also use it as a form of escapism from other sexual challenges. It poses problem when it becomes a substitute for relationship in which it becomes a

74

wasted love. The psychologist Kelsey observes that it can silence the urging of the spirit that invites a person to loving relationships and abort the opportunity for growth, this is the real sin masturbation according to the author.

Many people struggle with it and can be helped to reduce the tension it causes in their life and ministry. Self-care which consists in developing interest in some interesting activities, engaging in meaningful recreation, resting and relaxing as well as eating healthily. These activities help in keeping the stress and tension level under control so that they do not trigger the urge or the impulse to masturbate in the individual. It is also good that one identifies the circumstances which trigger that and avoid it. Those who are the 'digital natives', who expose themselves excessively to sexual stimuli, or those who patronize pornography suffer more in this regard. They masturbate with high frequency. Psychotherapy helps to cope with it.

c. Affective Dependence

This implies a consistent quest for a reassuring affection and seeking for affection in a disproportionate manner. Here there is a regression whereby the celibate returns artificially to the past, trying to bring the pleasures and experiences of the past into the present which is no longer adaptable. The person becomes dependent affectively-wise. This is demonstrated in undue falling in and out of love, seeking for confirmation to fill in some empty spaces in the mind or to cope with some failures and disappointments in life.

AIDS TO PSYCHOSEXUAL INTEGRATION

i. Prayer and Contemplation

Personal commitment to prayer is an imperative for living out celibacy. A fruitful and joyful celibate life is impossible without a personal communion with the Lord in prayer. Faithfulness to daily contemplative prayer or Eucharistic adoration (at least an hour) is helpful and supportive. Prayer here is not as an obligation or a mere routine, but prayer as an intense desire and longing to be with Him. It is an invitation to be and listen to Him. Celibacy requires an active prayer life to sustain it. It is through prayer that one draws the strength to keep both the bodily and sexual pleasures under control. From prayer, the celibate draws the spiritual strength for expressing genuine love and compassion. He or she also draws the inner strength for executing one's responsibility. A good prayer life constantly draws a person to the sacrament of reconciliation. With this, the person gains hope even in moments of desolation due to some scars from the weaknesses associated with the practicality of celibate chastity. This sacrament of reconciliation helps the person to develop a more delicate and sensitive conscience that abhors sins, especially the sin of impurity.

ii. Practice of Ascetism and Mortification

Every choice in life requires a great deal of discipline to sustain it. This entails both bodily and mental discipline. A married man or woman will have to acquire the virtue of discipline to keep to the partner especially in the sphere of sexual life. In the life of the celibate, it is no longer only discipline but the virtue of ascetism and some degrees of mortification. This consists in denying the self of little pleasures, for example in matters of appetite deferring a cup of coffee, taking a slice of bread when the body desires two slices, etc, these help to train the body not to have all it desires at all time. In the work area, it could be helping another fellow who is choked up with time to finish the workload; in spiritual sphere it could be praying more, kneeling more than before during prayers etc. Asceticism which is a decision to live a simple life (moderation in the use of social media, being duty-conscious at all cost, punctuality, accepting the work condition and people around oneself without discrimination, etc.) is a good aid in the psychosexual integration. It is an ascetical spirit that acts as the sustaining power. It helps the person to make mature daily choices, gaining the capacity to let go of pleasures which are not in line with one's value.

iii. Acceptance and not Repression of Sexual Feelings

This acceptance does not mean indulging in the sexual act. It rather means that one is aware of the inner state of both the body and the mind. It is with this awareness that one can control what is not acceptable to execute. Acceptance of the sexual feelings is the beginning of a healthy approach towards sexual maturity. This acceptance also helps a priest or religious to handle male/female attractions and some related issues. Acceptance helps to reduce some illusions for one recognizes that some of the truths or assumptions he or she have had in the past about oneself is false. For example, some believing they can watch pornography without being susceptible to its influence, or that they can sleep with the opposite sex (to whom they are attracted) without any indecent behaviour. At the realisation of the truth, one is therefore challenged to give up those idealized fantasies. It is only in this way that one is confronted with one's vulnerabilities and fragilities. One therefore makes a self-definition regarding one's choice of life and its credibility.

On the other hand, repressing sexual feelings is a block to sexual integration. It entails that one is not in touch with his or her feelings and therefore with reality. In this case, the individual is not at home discussing any sexual matters either about himself or about others. He or she has extracted anything sexual from the psyche. Oftentimes, people judge this type of person as a disciplined person or as one who has self-control. They fail to understand that the repressed feelings or emotions eventually surge up in a different form, this time in an unhealthy and undignified manner. This attitude is mainly observed in the intellectuals, those who have exchanged their leisure for work and those who think that the 'head' is enough to manage the internal affairs of the complexity of the human nature.

iv. Developing Sexual Boundaries

Every priest and religious will have to consciously draw a line around oneself regarding how he or she sends out and receives sexual messages both in spoken and unspoken manners. This is called sexual boundary. Physical boundary is very important. Psychic hygiene helps to maintain the physical boundary. Psychic hygiene entails keeping the mind and heart pure, free from pornographic images that may be replayed later. One must bear in mind that the heart does not desire what the eyes have not seen (*Quod oculus non videt, cor non desiderat*). This responsibility lies on the priest or the religious who is faced with a lifestyle of celibate chastity. He or she has the duty of maintaining appropriate emotional boundaries in the workplace and in the context of his or her apostolate, and through a disciplined life ensure that the co-workers are not allowed either to trespass or violate the boundaries. Friendships with people by the celibate will be more life-giving and a means of reaching God so long as the boundaries are kept. Therefore, the celibate must always leave a space for God in all relationships.

Involving in an exclusive relationship, short of marriage within the context of one's ministry or apostolate even when there is a mutual consent is not helpful. It is unethical. One must responsibly handle one's attraction and sexual fantasies without allowing them to be a block to the work of God. When sexual boundaries are created, they are as well communicated and kept. In this way, the question of crossing or violation of a boundary will not arise. Nevertheless, boundaries (including professional boundary) should not be too rigid or too porous. This does not favour apostolic effectiveness. Therefore, the priest or religious is to be flexible, ready and willing to break some boundaries in matters of charity.

v. Developing and Sustaining Celibate Friendships

When friendships are genuine and authentic, they become great pathway to celibate maturity. Healthy relationship whether same-sex or heterosexual is a great instrument in the deepening of one's affective life, without which relationship with God becomes more difficult. Friendship is a gift from the Lord. A celibate must always pray for this gift. Good friends facilitate sexual integration and help one to relate better with Jesus in his rational and emotional nature. In fact, Wanner maintains that "the development of friendship is a development of the spiritual life. When friendship is true, it can be one of the greatest ways in which God comes"[73]. A good friend helps the celibate to be in touch with himself or herself, face the realities of the strength and weakness of human nature and to develop those human qualities required in the ministry. In line with this, Parappully Jose believes strongly that "it is through genuine and integrated experience of intimacy that those qualities basic to ministry – gentleness, compassion, sensitivity and warmth – come to fruition in us"[74]. Despite the challenges and limitations of intimate friendship, it is a great support system for the celibate.

However, there should be consciousness on the part of the priest or religious, bearing in mind that heterosexual relationships may lead to a certain degree of exclusivity. It can hold one in captivity. In its negativity, it can therefore inhibit a person from total self-giving to God in love. For this reason, it is better to establish relationship with those who have the same values, those who are called to similar life commitments and therefore those who have also the desire and intention to love God with undivided attention.

Hakenewerth suggests six indications that a friendship is not healthy for the celibate. According to him, when:

- the expression of love seeks or demands genital involment;
- one or both friends resent the sharing of friendship with others;
- one considers the other person as belonging to him or her (possessiveness) and feels bound to regard the other as the Number One person in his or her life;
- one begins to expect or demand certain specific responses;
- one's commitment to the members of his or her religious community suffers because of their emotional involvement; and
- the friendship causes loss of interest in prayer.

Evaluate yourself!

[73] Wanner, R. 1987. *Aelred of Rievaulx: Twelfth Century Answers to Twentieth Century Questions*. Review for Religious, 46 (6), p. 923.

[74] Parappully, Jose and Jose Kuttianmattathil. 2012, p. 543.

vi. Developing Passion for One's Ministry or Apostolate

Being a priest or a religious offer them graceful opportunities to meet and interact with people. As stated earlier that part of celibacy is freedom in loving people, priests and religious through their work will relate with people selflessly. When there is great passion and zeal for one's work to the extent that one is consumed by the fire of love, by the fire of desiring to do what is good for the other, by the desire to relieve the other person's pain, etc, there will be little space left indeed for selfish love which is the antithesis of celibate chastity. When people experience the love and passion with which priests and religious care for them, they cannot but love and care for them in return. With this, loneliness has little space as well in the life of the celibate. Working with love and beyond the call of duty is helpful. Passion in one's ministry helps the person to inculcate a high degree of responsibility in the work entrusted to him or her. It helps the person to take initiative when necessary without over depending on the higher authority. With this, the person excels both in planning and execution of some projects for the good of all.

vii. Consulting a Good Spiritual Guide

Occasionally, the celibate will need to unload his or her worries, anxieties, fears, challenges with a person, and to process them. This exercise is not just done with anybody or anywhere. It must be within a circle of confidence and trust. A spiritual director helps the celibate to interpret his or her sexual challenges in the light of faith and in view of his or her Christian calling. The spiritual director offers some helpful insights to the person and adds meaning and hope to the person's life. Certain levels of surprises and confusion in the life of the celibate like falling in love or an abrupt interruption of a meaningful relationship are clarified, and spiritual insights helps the person to forge ahead. Withdrawing from an active life for a while into a more recollective session of about an hour to talk about these experiences is encouraging and indeed rewarding. It helps one to see his or her dynamics and where God is leading him or her to. A good spiritual guide uses his or her competency to relieve and elevate his clients. Indeed, part of psychosexual maturity is the capacity to discuss about one's sexual life and be sincere about it. In this, the person is helped to understand that one's body is not an obstacle to spiritual growth.

HEALTHY RELATIONSHIP

Many celibates engage in positive and fruitful friendships which act as support in their ministry. The deep spiritual communion and favour which most of them enjoy flow from their healthy relationship with others in the apostolate and ministry, for relating with people in a sincere manner facilitates doing that with God. This makes their friendships generative, embracing as many as the people of God in their circle of friendship. However, to some, issues of relationship still bother them. While some are disposed to gracefully embrace friends, some are not interested, but rather live a secluded and isolated life, and are incapable of dialogue.

While a thing can be possessed, a person cannot, ... the human person is not in full possession of himself but can find himself always and only in another and, finally in an Other.

IMODA FRANCO

In healthy relationship, the celibate is faithful and committed to his or her covenant of love with Christ. It is this commitment that sustains the consciousness of first belonging to Christ whole and entire, body and spirit, before belonging to the friend. Therefore, any form of possessive behaviour becomes out of place. Concerning this, Imoda stressed that "while a thing can be possessed, a person cannot, ... the human person is not in full possession of himself but can find himself always and only in another and, finally in an Other"[75]. One must be free to love. Genuine friendship thrives in altruism, so that sharing does not mean losing

---

[75] Imoda, Franco. 2007, 189.

and does not diminish what one has either in terms of spiritual, material or affection. It rather increases the capacity to love and appreciate the other. In a healthy relationship, the primary motivation is sincere love which is simply "the will to extend one's self for the purpose of nurturing one's own or another's spiritual growth"[76]. It does not depend on interdependence theory of costs and rewards, whereby a relationship is based on what one gains or what he or she loses. No. Priests and religious are called to love in the way Christ loved us – agape love. Caring for one another in different capacities, enjoying quality time together, giving one another space for one's philosophy of life, remembering one another's birthdays and anniversaries, dialoguing, forgiveness, truthfulness, tenderness and fraternal corrections are some of the qualities that sustain healthy relationship.

A healthy relationship is not without its challenges since the human heart battles with the desire for a marital mate. It is natural for men and women to date and have romantic feelings, but the celibate must make effort to avoid a dating mentality in the sense of the world which eventually metamorphizes into a third way style of life. It is a very challenging phenomenon among priests and religious. Attention should be paid to a mentality that seeks to date with romantic exclusivism which disrupts one's relationship with God. It is good to mention that the choice of healthy friendship is not a norm or value in the world of today. As such both the society and one's friends may not support the style of genuine love and healthy friendship. In this case, it is one's values and moral principles that should sustain the relationship. As Schneiders affirms as well, "when the social context does not support one's choices, personal motivation must be proportionately better-based and stronger"[77]. The celibate must be motivated by his or her strong belief system rooted in the

[76] Peck, Scott M. 2003. *The Road Less Travelled. A New Psychology of Love, Traditional Values and Spiritual Growth. 25th Anniversary Edition.* NY: Touchstone, p. 81.

[77] Schneiders, Sandra M. 2001. *Selling All. Commitment, Consecrated Celibacy, and Community in Catholic Religious Life.* NJ: Paulist Press, p. 131.

gospel value which he or she freely chooses to adopt as an ultimate way of life.

Having at least one close friend helps in one's mental stability and prevents one from all forms of psychosomatic sicknesses. In fact, there is a correlation between having good friends and good mental and spiritual balance. Unhealthy and negative friendships are enemies of mental and spiritual balance. Again, it is a mature attitude that people assert when a relationship is no longer healthy or fruitful. Sometimes friendships soar and haunt one. To this, those involved may either decide to allow it to die a natural death or disengage themselves from such relationship. Often, there is that romanticized ideology that friendship should not be ended, even when it causes one distress and a significant setback in one's ministry. Some people call this perseverance rather than admitting their poor judgement. No matter how painful it could be, adults are to accept the reality of admitting that a relationship is no longer helpful and therefore must end. Though painful are such experiences, but a mature mind will always forgive and 'let go'.

a. Responsible use of Freedom

The word freedom gives the impression of 'do as I like', especially to the youths. Priests and religious do not live in a different planet. It is good to understand that freedom entails responsibility as well and does not imply doing away with all forms of restrictions, or external coercion like social ethics or moral obligations. The influence of the unconscious can diminish the moral responsibility of an individual so that it becomes difficult for one to make an objective choice or to respond generously to God. However, one is responsible for the position one takes or refuses to accept. Because, the presence of the "unconscious does not determine any passive resignation with a negation of responsibility, but a redefining of responsibility"[78].

---

[78] Cencini, Amaedo R, and Alessandro Manenti. 2010, p. 271.

Freedom not only entails assuming one's responsibility, but more so, rejecting the responsibility that does not belong to one. Some priests and religious fall prey to this. They assume many responsibilities that are not theirs and therefore, put their ministerial life in jeopardy. By responsibility in this context, I mean our ability to own up and take responsibility for our actions, words and deeds irrespective of what causes them, be they outside or inside stimulus.

Freedom also implies the capacity to make decision according to one's conscience and making right moral choices. Karl Rahner strongly believes that one cannot boast of being free if he or she lacks the capacity to make decision. Taking decision implies giving up possibilities and one must be free of inordinate attachments to 'let go' of some choices.

The virtue of truth is important to developing true freedom. Contingent self-esteem is the primary motivation of actions here through some regulatory processes which are not integrated[79]. Suffice it to say that healthy self-esteem is needed for true freedom. This enables one to admit the truth always knowing that he or she loses nothing by saying what he or she feels or thinks (when necessary and required), for this does not diminish his or her self-worth.

The aspect of moral conscience is vital to the concept of freedom. Hence, freedom of conscience reminds one that one is free through one's will to accomplish good or avoid evil, she is in the grade of doing some necessary acts for her integral salvation. There is the need for interior education of the conscience, to live reconciled with oneself and with others in one's right conscience.

---

[79]   Deci, Edward L., and Richard M. Ryan. 1995, p. 39.

84

Chapter Four

UNDERSTANDING, ELABORATING EMOTIONS FOR POSITIVE WELL-BEING

Aware of the fact that emotions give meaning and vigour to actions, the chapter will discuss in detail the phenomenology of emotion. The aim is to understand the need to bring reason into feeling and vice-versa, and to harmonize both. This will help individuals to understand some natural and neurological *givens* and influences in their lives, for emotions are indeed tools of deepest awareness which help to progress as an integral being and as a functional person[80]. Aware that some people are emotionally inhibited, and therefore subject to emotional distress, it becomes important that they are aware of this. The chapter goes on to discuss the role of attachment in the affective development of the self. Correspondingly, secure attachment contributes to healthy development of the affect in a person. It renders one capable of mature relationship while insecure attachment distorts this capacity. It also shows the influence of nature and the environment in which one lives. Finally, the chapter will discuss the importance of psychological separation of the self as it produces internal freedom.

The word 'emotion' takes its origin from the Latin verb *motere,* which means "*to move*", plus the prefix "*e*" to connote "*move away*", suggesting that a tendency to act is implicit in every emotion[81]". It carries along a kind of motivational energy which becomes obvious in the actual action that the individual eventually performs. It is as if the person is compelled to act, even if not physically, but inwardly

---

[80] McLaren, Karla. 2010. *The Language of Emotions. What Your Feelings are Trying to Tell You.* Louisville, CO: Sounds True, p. 3.

[81] Goleman, Daniel. 2005, p. 6.

something is happening. This suggests that emotion is related to actions. Feeling precedes actions. Emotions have a "chameleonic nature" as it changes with environment and in concrete situations. This may have an object or can be because of imagination.

Different people feel and express emotions differently and with varying intensity. Not all experiences are communicable by words, and some experiences are better communicated through emotions. A gentle smile automatically conveys love and acceptance to the other. This explains why some gestures or signals concretise some feelings. Biological factors play a vital role both in acknowledging and expression of emotions. They contribute to either affective flattening or emotional blindness. For example, the removal of the amygdala through a surgical operation could result to affective blindness. This causes an attitude of disinterestedness in people. The danger becomes that of withdrawal and isolation. This is because the amygdala acts as a storehouse of emotional memory, and thus of significance itself; life without the amygdala is a life stripped of personal meanings[82]. The role of the amygdala is pivotal to emotional life.

According to Lewis, early emotions are rooted in the biological process, but the whole emotional life is embedded in the child's social and cognitive development which gives the necessary organic form its content and meaning. The emergence of consciousness produces the self-conscious emotions. Lewis argued that "emotional development is dependent on the emergence of consciousness, the self-conscious emotions"[83]. One is aware of her emotions as soon as she develops consciousness, this gives rise firstly to self-conscious emotions. For example, pride, which has direct reference to oneself appears by the second year of life. The standard rules or goals of the immediate family or even the environment instils this automatically in the child. The child tries to internalise them and adopt them into his/her system.

---

[82] Goleman Daniel. 2005, p. 15.

[83] Lewis, Michael, Jeannette M. Haviland-Jones, and Lisa. F. Barrett. 2008. *Hand Book of Emotions*. NY: Guilford Press, p. 279.

The model and definition of emotions by the author, Arnold, captures and situates emotion very well in interpersonal setting. According to him, emotions are mere tendencies to action but do not always lead to action. It is "the felt tendency toward anything intuitively appraised as good (beneficial), or away from anything intuitively appraised as bad (harmful). This attraction or aversion is accompanied by a pattern of physiological changes organised toward approach or withdrawal. The patterns differ for different emotions"[84]. They help in the judgement of the object. In other words, an object is always involved or a situation or an experience. Thus:

> Emotions are messages from our instinctive selves. They are important carriers of absolute (and often unwanted) truth. Although many emotions aren't welcome in most psyches, each of them has an indispensable function and something meaningful and precise to say. If we ignore and repress an emotion, we won't erase its message – we'll just shoot the messenger and interfere with an important natural process. The unconscious then has two choices: to increase the intensity of the emotion and present it to us one more time, or to give up on us and stuff the emotional energy deep into our psyches[85].

ORIGIN AND SOURCES OF EMOTIONS

Appraisal theory holds that emotions are elicited by evaluations (appraisals) of events and situations. For example, grief felt over the death of a beloved one is elicited by the evaluation of the fact that it is an irreparable loss. In other words, emotion is experience and situation centred. There must be the presence of a stimulus or experience for emotion to occur. It is the intensity of the experience that elicits emotions. The significant contribution of the appraisal theory is that people understand and interpret the experiences in relation to

---

[84] Arnold, Magda B. 1969. "Human Emotion and Action". Pp. 54-60 in *Human Action. Conceptual and Empirical Issues*, edited by T. Mitchel. NY: Academic Press.

[85] Arnold, Magda B. 1967, p. 191.

their present needs and goals. They also consider their ability to cope with the outcomes of these emotions[86]. So that the one who mourns interprets the emotion considering the challenges he or she will undergo because of the loss and the capacity to cope with it. The same thing applies to other emotions especially the primary ones.

In line with this, Mullaney attributes the underlying cause of emotion to be the stimulus of love. According to him, "all human emotions are derivations, reflections, and expressions of love, love-positive or love-negative, love gained, or love lost, love threatened, or love reassured, love rejected, or love restored, authentic love or pseudo-love, love hurt, or love healed. All emotions are generated by love and all are ordered to and aimed at bringing about the same end – love given and received[87]". Suffice it to say that every emotion is a product of an expression of the universal need to love and be loved. Whenever this need is thwarted in any form, it arouses different emotions in people. For instance, a deprivation of love may produce anger in some people or provoke hatred or embarrassment depending on the degree of ego weakness. Although the psycho-analysts maintain that the unconscious is the deepest element of being, Mullaney retains the heart to be the deepest. The table below explains better the author's sources of emotion as coming from the intrinsic need of love[88].

When my love is...	*Love's response is...*	*Because love's goal and need is always...*
Hurt, treated unjustly by someone	Anger	Restoration of justice, the measure of love's inalienable rights/needs

---

[86] Davidson, Richard J., Klaus R. Scherer, and Hill H. Goldsmith. 2003. *The Handbook of Affective Sciences*. NY: Oxford University Press, p. 564.

[87] Mullaney, Brennan J. 2008. *Authentic Love. Theory and Therapy*. NY: Society of St. Paul, p. 65.

[88] Mullaney, Brennan J. 2008, p. 70.

Violated by my own sin (my abuse of my own love standards and integrity)	Guilt	Honouring the command of conscience for a clean heart-openness, honesty
Overtly threatened, physically or emotionally, by a visible danger to love	Fear	Life – the enduring wholeness of love of self and others
Covertly threatened by an undefined danger to the heart (injury to love of self or others)	Anxiety	Same as above
Threatened with annihilation, destruction at the deepest core of the heart	Angst, panic	Same as above, compounded by the mistaken belief that love can ever be totally destroyed.
Vested and projected into the future as a promise of love's continuing existence	Hope	Eternal life. (Hope is an integral component of all authentic love)
Misused (by myself) as an expression of pseudo-power	Unjustified anger, abusiveness	Realization of authentic power which, in abuse, derives from pseudo-love.

The heart is the deepest and the most sensitive part of the human person. The most painful and delicate experiences are in the heart and not in the brain. Love is what motivates all emotions, and this is so because everyone craves for love, all wish to love and be loved. A baby that has everything needed for survival but lacks love, that simple smile, cuddling, caressing, pecking, reassurance, etc., naturally dies off.

THE MECHANISM OF EMOTIONS

Emotions can come about from one's perception. Sometimes perception is not very exact. There can be some incongruence in perception and that ends up producing false emotions and experiences. Davidson is in support of this view when he said that "people's emotion arises from their perceptions of their circumstances-immediate, imagined, or remembered"[89]. Emotions occur systematically. First, there is an appraisal, that is, we recognise something as good or bad. This determines if we are to approach or move away from the object or scenario. For example, the presence of a loved one automatically pulls one towards the direction of the person by increasing the 'pleasure appetite'. The presence of an enemy can make one to change direction. It implies that emotions are evaluatively subjective most of the time since it is based on the individual's interpretation concerning the person's mental state.

Arnold argued that "to arouse an emotion, the object must be appraised as affecting me in some way, affecting me personally as an individual with my particular experience and my particular aims"[90]. The arousal carries along with it either attraction or repulsion which is not merely a physiological state. For example, anger instils in a person an impulse to defend the self through some *acting outs*, like shouting or fighting. The sound of melodious psalms by the Novices can serve as an external stimulus and may trigger emotions of joy, or serenity or even anger depending on one's disposition. Internal stimulus is difficult to dictate, it is peculiar to the physiological aspects and probably disposition of the individual. The will decides the expression of these emotions so long as the person is emotionally free and has no history of brain injury, or any other sickness which disturbs the will from its function. Whenever an episode that carries along with it some emotions occurs in one's life, it reminds the person of a similar experience in the past. Arnold refers to this as af-

[89] Davidson, Richard J., Klaus R. Scherer, and Hill H. Goldsmith. 2003, p. 572.
[90] Arnold, Magda B. 1960, 171.

fective memory. This is spontaneous and unstructured in the psyche. The previous impulse is brought back to the here and now, either a positive or a negative experience. Consequently, the residue of previous emotion returns. When an emotional experience repeats itself severally, it may elicit the same effect which may be more intense[91].

We shall briefly explore some emotions which occur in daily interpersonal relationships. The chapter concentrates on the primary and self-conscious emotions. The aim is that a knowledge of these emotions will enhance constructive emotional episodes rather than destructive ones.

EXPLORING THE SELF-CONSCIOUS EMOTIONS

The self-conscious emotions peculiarly involve the self. They help in the evaluation of one's capacity to establish stable self-representations. This helps in the evaluation of oneself about one's internal and external value system. The self and emotion are inseparable. Self-conscious emotions are central to motivating and regulating people's behaviour, especially thoughts and feelings. These emotions can be elicited mainly in the cognitive domain. Nevertheless, most authors have found out that there is no constant elicitor of these self-conscious emotions, and there is no cause-and-effect pattern either. The self-conscious emotions which we shall consider here are shame, guilt, pride, and embarrassment.

a. The Emotion of Shame

Shame is an acute social emotion which draws the attention of a person to his or her social limits. This generates the reluctance to act beyond those limits[92]. Somehow it reminds one of the interior deficiencies and unworthiness. The defect might be real or imagined especially in the case of those who naturally feel inferior. Ordinarily, the experience of failure typically elicits the emotion of shame.

---

[91] Arnold, Magda B. 1969, p. 173-174.

[92] Ellison, Carol R. 2000, p. 27.

92

There is a self-diminishing effect whenever there is a failure to meet up with a desired goal or standard. It is even more difficult when this goal or standard is made known to the public. The need for success triggers this emotion. In this case, the one experiences a lot of anxiety which leads to isolation, withdrawal, and avoidance of others. It affects the self-worth of the person especially in the codependents who devalue and underestimate themselves due to their ego weakness and low anxiety tolerance.

In her effort to explain the emotion of shame, McLaren departs by defining 'shamelessness'. According to her, while shame is an outcome of guilt and doing wrong; and the consequence of not measuring up to one's standard in life, shamelessness on the other hand is to be "senseless, uncouth, and impudent. It is a very marked state of being out of control, out of touch, and exceedingly self-absorbed; therefore, shamelessness lives only in people who don't have any relational skills[93]". It implies that those who lack interpersonal intelligence experience more of this emotion. This is because shame occurs in the context of an interpersonal relationship. It is due to breaking one's boundary from inside. It is also a moral and social value since it reminds one of the transgressions.

Moreover, shame has some positive contributions as it is a social value. It helps in the regulation of one's life. It may also lead to deep spiritual and religious experience. For example, if one who transgressed socially is asked to read an apology letter publicly, or other form of such humiliating activity. The experience brings down the self-worth of the person to an extent and brings sadness and depression. But it may also lead to a spiritual encounter and subsequently to a change of attitude and behaviour.

b. The Emotion of Guilt

When people attribute their failures to their irresponsibility and lack of diligence in carrying out their duties, guilt sets in. Naturally,

---

[93] McLaren, Karla. 2010, p. 197-199.

people feel pain for their negligence and assign a cause to it. Guilt occurs because of an acceptance of one's failure to uphold or actualise his or her standards, rules, and goals of life. The emotion is not as intense as shame which occurs mainly in the social context. In other words, it does not affect so much the self-esteem of the person. It concerns failure in a specific action and not on the person[94]. It is the regret one nurtures for a wrong act or deed. This is because as the individual is convinced of his or her contributions to the failure, the self is pushed towards repair. Therefore, the emotion of guilt carries with it some level of corrective therapy. It aids the individual to evolve into a more conscious, reflective, and moral being. It even provides the person with the moral strength for introspective supervision of one's character without either exaggeration or devaluation of the self.

Moral transgression leads to guilt. Guilt is related to the spiritual functions of the person. It helps in the evaluation of the person's action within the group, to know if it is progressive or destructive. Religious men and women have an unusual propensity to feel guilty for transgressing God's law and that of the community. This may lead to anxiety which is attributed to the fear of social, cultural as well as divine retribution. It also awakens spiritual consciousness. However, without the capacity of reflection, guilt will be of no positive effect. Only normal guilt which gears towards moral and sociocultural responsibility of a person can lead to corrective emotional experience. Neurotic guilt which centres on the fear of what others think or perceive in relation to a negative action is never fruitful.

c. The Emotion of Pride

Pride being a self-conscious emotion is one of the most challenging emotions among priests and religious. It is an emotion generated by appraisals that one is responsible for a socially valued outcome or for being a socially valued person. It is achievement-oriented emotion and gives more confidence to the person. It is a

---

[94] Lewis, Michael, Jeannette M. Haviland-Jones, and Lisa. F. Barrett. 2008. *Hand Book of Emotions*. NY: Guilford Press, p. 805.

94

sense of fulfilment in seeing one's effort or labour come to actualization. Consistent with this perspective, Lewis reiterates that "pride is
the consequence of a successful evaluation of a specific action[95]". It
implies that before this emotion, there is first, an input of something
which eventually gives birth to the feeling. This can be in the form
of physical or intellectual hard work. One becomes fulfilled for the
much he or she can put in.

Au and Canon named a type of pride which is found mainly among
priests and religious as perfectionistic pride. Perfectionistic individuals
fall prey to this. This is due to their self-righteousness in which the self
unconsciously seeks "to establish itself with God on the basis of its
own achievement[96]". The person thinks he or she can achieve holiness
based on self-efforts or natural endowments. This makes the self-prone
to constant self-criticisms in the face of failures and mistakes, and consequently to self-condemnation. This leads to constant guilt.

Furthermore, pride has two facets, hubristic and authentic pride
which mirror shame and guilt. Hubristic pride like shame results
from internal, stable, uncontrollable and global attributions. It is a
direct attention to the self which produces self-aggrandisement and
conceit. In hubristic pride, the subject and object are fused. Here,
there is the inability to identify one's limitations. In hubris, there is
arrogance and false evaluation of the self, while authentic pride is
marked with humility[97]. For example, with success, a person with
hubris can say, "I attained success because I am a great person",
whereas one with authentic pride is likely to say, "I attained success
because I worked hard and put in my best". There is a false evaluation of the self. Suffice it to say that hubris is simply an overestimation of self-confidence or an inflated ego. It is a result of evaluation
of success in relation to some standard rules and regulations with the
focus on the global self.

---

[95] Lewis, Michael, Jeannette M. Haviland-Jones, and Lisa. F. Barrett. 2008, p. 749.

[96] Au, Wilkie., and Noreen Cannon. 1995, p. 73.

[97] Lewis, Michael, Jeannette M. Haviland-Jones, and Lisa. F. Barrett. 2008, p. 889.

d. The Emotion of Embarrassment

The need for recognition and affirmation is universal to all people of all cultures. Not recognising one's effort is unpleasant. More unpleasant is discrediting one's effort or image in the presence of the other. This brings about the emotion of embarrassment. It "requires appraisals of identity-goal relevance, identity-goal incongruence, and internal attributions[98]". Embarrassment is closely related to shame but differs on the level of intensity. It is milder than shame and does not involve a disequilibrium of thoughts. Mainly people use reaction formation to cope with this emotion. Usually, this emotion takes place in the context of an interpersonal relationship. Some authors classify embarrassment as 'a form of social anxiety'. It occurs when people perceive that attention is on them and that others discredit and devalue them. When there is a comparison of others and one feels judged by the high standards or criteria of others. It carries along with it some physiological changes like heartbeats and frowning of the face. The need for social approval from others, fear of negative evaluation, being more self-conscious, or being introverted might influence levels of embarrassability.

EXPLORING SOME OF THE BASIC EMOTIONS OF THE SELF

a. The Emotion of Anger

Anger is an automatic response to physical or emotional pain. It does not occur in isolation but always regarding painful feelings. It carries with it some physiological signs like the change of the colour of the face. Some internal symptoms could be the flow of blood to the hands, which facilitates the strong urge to use a weapon as a coping mechanism. There is an increase in the heartbeat as well as that of hormones like adrenaline[99]. According to neo-behaviourists, anger is

---

[98] Lewis, Michael, Jeannette M. Haviland-Jones, and Lisa. F. Barrett. 2008, p. 889.

[99] Goleman, Daniel. 2005, p. 6.

caused by omitting the positive reinforcers. It can also be caused when one's goal or expectations are frustrated or thwarted. This may result to fight or flight attempt or motivation. If the person is motivated to fight, the result will be anger. Using cognitive appraisal approach, it is not the situation that causes the emotion but the way the individual interprets it. According to this theory, "anger is an unpleasant emotion that often occurs in response to an appraisal of a blocked goal"[100]. This could lead to an obstruction in reaching one's goal or even make punishment present and possible. Anger can also be primarily due to a physical harm, or as a result of thwarting one's needs and wants, or a threat to one's self-esteem, or by injustice. In every case, it is a precondition for both intra and inter personal conflict. It is present in one's daily experiences and an aspect of all relationships.

Though anger is always characterised as a negative emotion, since it is an integral part of aggression, hostility, and violence, it can also have the apparent function of energizing the person for defence. It can therefore, be positive as well. This is because anger is "a conflictive emotion that is biologically related to aggressive systems and social living, symbolization and self-awareness. Psychologically it is aimed at the correction of a perceived wrong and sociocultural at upholding accepted standards of conducts"[101]. In this case, anger becomes somehow beneficial.

For priests and religious in the ministry, the challenge is to integrate anger in their lives, to accept this emotion as a normal and positive force which can contribute to self-awareness and self-understanding, rather than seeing it as a threat to life. By tracing the root of anger and accepting that the causes of anger are not external (the external factors act just as stimulus), one is fortified and disposed to a constructive expression of anger.

---

[100] Lewis, Michael, Jeannette M. Haviland-Jones, and Lisa. F. Barrett. 2008 p. 775.

[101] Strongman, Kenneth T. 2003. *The Psychology of Emotion. From Everyday Life to Theory*. Fifth Edition. Chichester, U.K.: John Wiley and Sons Press, p. 133-134.

b. Emotion of Envy

Envy is one of the emotions that people do not want to be associated with, though it affects many, but it is seldom discussed and acknowledged. The root of the word *'envy'* is the Latin word *invidere* or *invidia,* meaning to look with malice or resentment...to begrudge. In other words, the envious person views things with an evil eye. Envy is based on the wrong understanding and perception that goodness is limited to a commodity. Therefore, the more another has this commodity, the less for the person who envies. The human person is naturally attracted to anything good. The heart desires the good and when it fails to achieve it, envy sets in. It is the despair of not possessing it that triggers envy at seeing another have it. This is also associated with the desire to destroy the one who seems to possess this advantage. The self becomes frustrated and consequently envious.

Buried in man's heart is the envy which most of the times is a quest or desire for wholeness or something which is frustrated or thwarted. Human beings feel an unconscious emptiness and vacuum. This void produces the intense desire and longing for fulfilment. Unaware that this emptiness can be fulfilled only by the Transcendent, the envious person is full of illusion by thinking he or she will complete himself or herself having acquired certain goods[102]. Masochism plays a lot here since the envier suffers more than the envied.

Envy is potentially rooted in all hearts though more profound and dominant in some personalities than others. It contributes to a large extent to misunderstandings among sisters in the community. In fact, beneath most group conflict is an unconscious envy by the individuals. No group or society can exist without the emotion of envy. This is because the disparity in natural endowments is inevitable. This may generate resentment, especially for those who are not yet psychologically separated. They feel unhappy and less worthy by other people's talents and gifts, and therefore look for flaws rather than appreciating the talents and achievements of others. Otherwise, different gifts and talents can be a source of richness for the

---

[102] Au, Wilkie., and Noreen Cannon. 1995, p. 81-83.

whole group or community when put together. It does not give one the room to acknowledge and affirm the good seen in others, instead it gives more room for criticisms. The major reason for envy stems from lack of gratitude for all the gifts and favours received from God and neighbours. Since they find it difficult to acknowledge and appreciate their own gifts and talents, they also do not actualise their many potentials.

c. The Emotion of Jealousy

Jealousy typically concerns what one possesses and fears losing it. It takes place in the context of a threat to a valued relationship. Therefore, it is a combination of fear and anger that arises in its mood state when one's most intimate and essential relationships are threatened. It points towards internal and external insecurity. There is the fear of abandonment, of not getting the affection and love needed from the loved and desired one. Infidelity and unfaithfulness are central to the cause of jealousy. When a partner in a relationship perceives this as a threat, fear of losing the connection and anger to the rivalry dominates. Hogg and Copper are in support of this when they maintain that a jealous episode is triggered by the perception of a relational threat, which activates jealousy-related cognitive appraisals and emotions[103].

However, this emotion should not be treated as a weed that must be uprooted from the garden to allow the vegetables grow. When accepted and integrated, it can be a source of growth and more profound love between the person and Jesus who is a jealous lover. It will help the individual to give undivided attention to Him. There is a sound healing knowledge that comes with jealousy. For jealousy is not always harmful and does not always have a negative effect. Sometimes it could be because of genuine love and affection[104]. It can also help a person to realise the extent to which the other cares for him or her.

---

[103] Hogg, Michael A., and Joel Cooper. 2007, p. 233.

[104] Spitzberg, Brian H., and William R. Cupach. 2010. *The Dark Side of Close Relationships*. NY: Lawrence Erlbaum Associates Publishers, p. 34.

d. The Emotion of Sadness

Everyone has some expectations in life. Many expect at least some minimum level of success in whatever they do. When the result is positive, it brings joy and happiness, but when the outcome is negative, the result is sadness. Therefore, it can easily be said that sadness is a consequence of appraisal of loss or failure. It is a resignation and acceptance of failure. Sadness does not occur in isolation. It is always relating to other emotions like anger and fear. Goleman observes that sadness "brings a drop-in energy and enthusiasm for life's activities, particularly diversions and pleasures, and, as it deepens and approaches depression, slows the body's metabolism. This introspective withdrawal creates the opportunity to mourn a loss or frustrated hope, grasp its consequences for one's life, and, as energy returns, plan new beginnings[105]". Unchecked sadness can lead to depression.

There are some psychological benefits of sadness. For notwithstanding the unpleasant mood that this emotion creates, it provides the individual with the opportunity of evaluating the experience or situation, and subsequent working through. Though it brings to consciousness one's painful state, it could also lead to mindfulness which is a definite adaptive process of growth of the self. Sadness can make one develop a kind of depth and lead to empathy and more understanding, or it can make one more vengeful. It can either lead to a positive or negative depth.

PROCESSING EMOTIONS AND FEELINGS

Feelings do not mean the same thing as emotions. While feelings are concerned with mainly the state of our body and its organs, emotions have to do with the reactions to the world around us and our inner psychic world. Emotion is like a catalyst that makes one ever ready to act or behave in accordance to situations. On the spiritual level, a good examination of conscience and consciousness

---

[105] Goleman, Daniel. 2005, p. 4.

are antidotes to emotional betrayals. This is because, during these processes, one can reflect and evaluate each episode of emotional encounter in an objective manner, thanks to the grace of God and the Spirit who enlightens man. Good knowledge of the lives of the saints leads to a strong attraction and consequently to the imitation of the saints. Eventually, this may lead to the acquisition of the value of self-control.

It is God who created human emotions and sentiments. With clarity on the concept of emotion, especially on its moral neutrality, individuals are more open to process their emotions. When it is rather understood as passion, individuals attribute it to their 'ego weakness' and therefore close up or shy away from it. As a result, they repress and suppress their emotions so that their lifestyles will tally with the dictum that "*ladies are to be seen not heard*", or "*men do not cry, be a man*". Suppression, repression and denial of emotions are sometimes understood as discipline and practice of virtue. As such, some priests and religious spiritualize their emotions. Everything is seen in the light of God's will and spirit of sacrifice. There is no need denying the reality. Suppression of unpleasant emotion and spiritualization are not helpful. If Jesus could weep (Cf. Jn.11:35); was angry (Cf. Mk.3:5); filled with joy (Cf. Lk. 10:21), was indignant (Cfr.Mk.10:21), it follows that those who aspire to follow Him more closely, and to replicate His sentiments in their apostolate and ministry can do the same as well. They should learn to express their emotions properly.

Consequently, McLaren maintains that "if we ignore or repress an emotion, we won't erase its message; we will just shoot the messenger and interfere with an important natural process. The residues of the emotional experiences remain. The unconscious has two choices: to increase the intensity of the emotion and present it to us one more time, or to give up on us and stuff the emotional energy deep into our psyches[106]". None of the options here is healthy; each choice will eventually lead to future compulsion or addiction or a

---

[106] McLaren, Karla. 2010, p. 31.

type of psychosomatic sickness. If this is so, there is the indispensable need to resort to a healthier way of expressing emotions.

A healthy expression of emotion begins with being aware of the emotion. Hence, one must be in touch with oneself as to notice some physiological changes like the heartbeat, dry mouth, and choking, depending on the emotion in question. There must be the ability to observe these changes in the body system. Secondly, when an emotion is noticed, a correct name should be allotted to it. For example, what is it I am feeling now? I feel sad, or happy? There is nothing that delights the heart as when a person's name is pronounced correctly. It has a positive effect in the psyche in disposing the individual to accept whatever message is coming. In the same vein, appropriating correct name to the emotion helps one to own the emotion up. An individual will handle his/her emotions better only when he/she has responsibly accepted them as belonging to him/her. For "a dialectic that is known and accepted is easier to manage than that which is unknown and not accepted"[107]. The tendency is always to shift it to others, "he or she made me feel jealous because of the exhibition of her talents", instead of admitting, "I feel jealous of her talents and the way she uses it positively, I wish I have such talents". In as much as the other may constitute the stimulus for the arousal of the emotion, still, the emotion can be personalized or not. There is no moral judgment. Therefore, I accept my jealously and my limitations in choosing.

In the processing of emotions, "the goal is balance, not emotional suppression: every feeling has its value and significance. A life without passion would be a dull wasteland of neutrality, cut off and isolated from the richness of life itself[108]". For when St Irenaeus said that *the glory of God is the man fully alive,* he was asserting that man in his activity and not passivity brings glory to God. Emotions are tools of our most profound awareness which leads to the whole functioning of the person. It leads one into a greater self-awareness which enables one to recognize the emotion at work.

---

[107] Kiely, Bartholomew M. 1987, p. 246

[108] Goleman, Daniel. 2005, p. 56.

A useful way of processing emotion is by developing the third dimension of the person. This consists in extra-curricular activities (sports, music, playing piano and gardening) which helps in making one less emotionally vulnerable. If one is internally safe, then he or she will not agitate or react to every little thing since he or she knows that the experience does not define him or her. Normally, those with an internal locus of control react less to emotional stimulus. They have a positive attitude which is constructed right from their infancy.

TRANSFORMING OUR EMOTIONS

In a network and circle of friends, one is bound to get hurt sometimes and to hurt some people as well. Even in some experiences, there is a deliberate decision to inflict pain and suffering on the other, or to humiliate the other. That is a natural phenomenon. It will be unnatural if it does not exist. Rolheiser contends that "any pain or tension that we do not transform we will transmit[109]". This holds for all the emotions. If one does not transform the emotion of anger, the result may be hitting the other person or vomiting some venoms. If one does not transform the emotion of envy and jealousy, the result will be bearing perpetual grudges. Not transforming one's emotion may result to passing electric currents of negative emotions to people.

The natural tendency and temptation when confronted with negative emotion is to react negatively. A kind of, 'you insulted me so I also insult you', period! But the answer remains always, what will Christ do in such situation? What will the Blessed Mother do? The whole gospel message lies in the invitation to go beyond the natural instincts, to allow grace to act and transform the human nature. In that case love transforms hatred, gratitude transforms envy, humility transforms embarrassment and so on. It is this aspect of transformation of one's emotions that gives the unique character of a Christian. The emphasis is on knowing when to act according to

---

[109] Rolheiser, Ronald. 2014, p. 251.

emotional drive. In this case Jesus and his Mother are the models. They know when to react and when to withdraw. St Theresa of the child Jesus is also a paradigm. Sometimes she would have water in her mouth to avoid over reacting (not that she never reacted). How one manages her emotions determines his or her level of affective maturity.

Chapter Five

TOWARDS A NEW HORIZON
OF AFFECTIVE MATURITY

Apart from the principles of aspects affective maturity already discussed, this chapter is concerned with other psychological approaches which are essential and helpful to developing maturity in the affective sphere. These include: the development of empathy, establishment of healthy boundaries, management of attractions, communication dynamics, conflict management and resolution.

THE HEALING POWER OF EMPATHY

There is nothing that joys the heart as one feeling understood before the other. The German psychologist Theodore Lipps coined the word "einfuhlung", which literally means, "in-feeling". He used it to describe the emotional appreciation of another's feelings. From there other psychologists took off. Empathy does not have the same meaning as sympathy. It differs from sympathy for the fact that the later does not last, in virtue of its being an emotional reaction, it is passive and often does not lead to action. For example, a boss may sympathize with her employee for working overtime, but few minutes later adds another word to the already existing one. On the other hand, empathy is lasting since it is an attitude a person adopts. It renders one more sensitive to the suffering of the other and leads to a positive action. Here the boss will put him/herself in the position of the employer who has already much to do, and therefore may decide to defer the work or help.

Empathy entails being tender hearted to people. Some neurologists and psychologists hold that people who are not able to be tender-hearted are so because of biological factors. Those who have damage to their right somatosensory cortices no longer can judge other's emotions, and consequently, have lost a skill that is crucial for empathy. Also, some are because of damage to the prefrontal cortex. When these biological dysfunctions are present, they lead to impairments in the appraisal of emotions and related constructs. Hence, there is a correlation between biological healthiness and the development and practice of empathy[110]. For one to practice empathy, the ego boundaries should be somewhat flexible. There must be a temporary breach of ego when it is necessary and adaptable. There must be regression for empathy to occur. The cognitive and affective processes must combine to produce an empathic behaviour. When the ego boundary is too rigid, individuals remain only at the intellectual level. In this case, people emphasize only rules, regulations and order without considering the feelings of the other. In fact, it is a flow of one's perception to affection.

Empathic attitude is an imperative in the apostolate and ministry of priests and religious. This entails trying to understand their collaborators in the Lord's vineyard in the here and now. It will also mean appreciating people's sensitivity and differentness. Priests and religious are to be emotionally attuned to all under their care, especially those working directly under them. There is no doubt, empathy is contagious. In being empathic, they will win many souls to Christ, even without standing at the pulpit to preach. This is because emotional awareness of the other is vital to the understanding of that person. In fact, it is difficult to understand the other if one does not put oneself in that person's shoe or see things from the other's point of view. When this is done in a psychological sense, one becomes aware of the emotions of other people.

Suppose you are sharing your experience with your friend about the treatment which you received from another fellow, and which makes you depressed. You are in tears pouring out your hearts. Your

---

[110] Lopez, Shane J., and Charles R. Snyder. 2007. *Positive Psychology. The Scientific and Practical Explorations of Human Strengths*. Oaks, CA: Sage Publications, p. 269.

heart is full of pain and sadness as you are sharing this bitter experience. To your greatest surprise your friend interrupted you by preaching to you that you should forget that, and that God's love for you is bigger than that of your friend (spiritualization). As you are trying to digest that, she continues by telling you that you should or supposed to understand that the person who treated you badly is under stress, and that his or her poor family upbringing contributes to his or her queer character, giving a wonderful analysis of how this affects him or her (rationalization). At the end, your friend says, "it's how you interpret it. Be positive, finish". This would make any healthy person more depressed. Not only you feel you were not understood, but you will also feel your friend also judged you, making you feel guilty of not understanding the person. These are facts but can never erase the feelings of the one who feels hurt.

This is the major problem of some priests and religious. The busy nature of the physical world and the internal fragmentations of the human heart make it difficult for people to really listen to one another. It is either they interrupt the speaker and rush to put things in order with series of preaching and advice, without trying to understand the person from his or her own worldview. Each of us requires to be understood as a unique entity with unique experience, otherwise all forms of advice or counselling or therapy becomes futile. Empathy means that the listener becomes influenced by the uniqueness of the speaker. This is what is called empathic listening. That is, listening with the motive to understand. It implies waving aside all forms of internal noise which makes the heart hypersensitive and always alert in preparation either to speak or to interpret. We do not understand others through our own lens or experiences, but through theirs. Unnecessary projections worsen the situation and makes the speaker to close more. It is not about trying to be understood by the other but trying to understand the other. It is for this that empathic people do not just listen with their ears for sounds or the spoken words, but more with their hearts and eyes, observing for feelings and gestures.

An empathic friend will calmly listen to the speaker with attention. Put himself or herself in the position of the speaker which helps to acknowledge that the experience is indeed painful. Respect the unique feelings of the speaker (compassion) and use some consoling words like, "I can understand how you feel", "it's really painful", "Oh, what a pain, you must have suffered as a result of this..." These are soothing words which are like balm or tranquilizer that helps the person to process the pains. Long sermons and intellectualizations worsen the situation. The wounded heart at that moment can be likened to a baby who cries to have a toy. Any lecture on why the baby should not have that toy at that time is unnecessary and waste of time. What the care-giver should do is to act as a surrogate mum, caress the baby and help her to relax and accept the reality. Not by many words.

ESTABLISHMENT OF HEALTHY BOUNDARIES

The importance of both psychological and physical boundaries cannot be overemphasized among priests and religious. It is this healthy boundary that helps in proper execution of one's duty. The processes of individuation and separation, attachment and bonding help in this. Boundaries exist to prevent bad elements like manipulation, intimidation and harassment which impede healthy relationship. A clear boundary helps in promoting one's integrity and wards off inappropriate behaviors. With healthy boundaries one guards one's ambitions, potentials and even the integrity and wholeness of one's relationships. A psychological boundary is like 'a membrane' that surrounds individual and each subsystem in the family. Like the membrane around a cell, boundary needs to be firm enough to ensure the integrity of the cell and yet sufficiently permeable to allow some level of communication between cells. The establishment of healthy ego boundaries produce a sense of personal identity which enables one to describe and define his or her relationships with others and with the external boundaries[111].

---

[111] Cencini, Amaedo, and Alessandro Manenti. 2010, p. 248.

Boundaries prevents both sexual and emotional abuse[112]. Despite the happy self-donation in celibacy, priests and religious are faced with the fiery force of sexuality. The limitations of human beings (including the celibates) is expressed in their unconscious search to be completed by another. This can only be possible by couples who are into marriage. And this need does not in any way respect anybody or any status. Therefore, priests must not be naïve or underrate the power of sexual instincts. Clear relational boundaries are protective. This is to avoid channelling the energy of the *eros* in an unhealthy manner.

Involving in an exclusive friendship within the context of one's ministry even when there is a mutual consent is not helpful. It is unethical. Naturally, intimate friendships both consciously and unconsciously yearn for closer and deeper modes of physical and genital expression. When those involved in friendship do not observe the boundaries, it is most likely that they may indulge in their sexual fantasies and impulses. One must responsibly handle one's attraction and sexual fantasies without allowing them to be a block to the work of God. When sexual boundaries are created, they are as well communicated to those concerned and kept. In this way, the question of crossing or violation of a boundary will not arise. Friendships with people by the celibate will be more life-giving and a means of reaching God so long as the boundaries are kept. Nevertheless, boundaries should not be too rigid or too porous. This does not favour apostolic effectiveness. Therefore, the priest or the religious is

---

[112] Emotional abuse 'humiliation and degradation, threatened or actual emotional or physical control and terrorization, threatened or actual emotional or physical rejection/neglect, social, social isolation, and exploitation'. EA of woman consists in 'the use of verbal and nonverbal acts that symbolically hurt a woman or (2) the use of threats about causing physical harm. Verbal act of emotional abuse include criticizing, making belittling remarks, screaming, and badgering. Nonverbal acts of emotional abuse include destroying personal belongings; emotionally or physically hurting a woman's family, friends, or pets; limiting access to resources such as money; and isolating a woman socially'. Cf. Levinson, Ponzetti and Jorgensen 1999: 215-216.

to be flexible, ready and willing to break some boundaries in matters of charity.

Different types of boundaries exist ranging from rigid, enmeshed and clear boundaries. Rigid boundaries are restrictive as it permits minimal contact between the priest or the sister and the collaborators or parishioners. This leads to superficial relationships. Consequently, transference becomes almost impossible. Although this may positively foster autonomy to an extent, it may also lead to a marked disengagement of the parishioners or other workers from the Church activities and related assignments. In all, rigid boundaries create a lot of stress. It renders the system poor in affection and emotional support which is a requirement for human formation[113]. It is good to note that if the boundaries are too rigid, it affects the interpersonal relationship among people as the affective state will be significantly affected. In this case, people need more intellectual energy to cope with the demands of their daily life. Therefore, working with or for priests and religious, or even collaboration among priests and his brother priests or sister with her fellow sisters becomes a cross. Rigid boundaries diminish the general output in any work setting.

Enmeshed boundaries offer closeness and support in an exaggerated manner so to say. In this case the priest or the religious offer a lot for his or her subjects or collaborators. As such, people find it difficult to operate independently and therefore lack competence in doing many things. Jordan notes that if the boundaries are enmeshed or diffused, there is the possibility that one may lose one's self-differentiation and thereby opening some avenues for uncontained attributes of narcissism. In this case, there is the indiscriminate and lawless attitude of both the formators and candidates. Things are taken for granted and regulations are easily rationalized away. In this, the genuine sense of human connectedness is given up easily

---

[113] Nichols, Michael P. 2010. *Family Therapy. Concepts and Methods*. Ninth Edition. NY: Pearson, p. 170-171.

and lost[114]. This is not helpful. A clear boundary is recommended for effective ministry. This enables people to interact freely with respect and some reservations. The boundary must be clear, conscious and purposeful. When these boundaries are appropriately observed, people work with less tension. Priests and religious are to avoid dual or overlapping role relationships, which may sometimes produce errors of judgment, biases, and distortions of objectivity. For example, a lady is both the cook in the convent or presbytery and the secretary at the office. So, she becomes both an insider and an outsider. Or a priest becomes the spiritual director of his house boy. Healthy ego boundaries help in establishing a personal identity which helps in shaping and defining relationships with others.

MANAGEMENT OF ATTRACTIONS

One of the major conflicts of the youth is that of handling different types of attractions. Attraction is a momentary state when a person experiences the elation or euphoria of inclination towards the other, with the desire to be with the person for the fulfilment of needs (both dissonant and consonant). However, it implies a positive evaluation from the one who feels attracted. Attraction, which is a usual and natural occurrence could interfere seriously with the normal routine of a person's life, especially romantic or sexual attractions. It has an adverse effect on the people's work.

Gray contends that women battle more with attractions towards friendship since they are naturally more emotional especially in the face of difficulty and problems while men are more detached. There is a continuous ongoing connection, dependence, and interdependence among creatures, not just among human beings for survival[115]. Proximity increases the possibility of attraction among people. This is because the interaction is with less difficulty and the parties are

---

[114] Jordan, Judith V., Alexandra G. Kaplan, Jean B. Miller, Irene P. Stiver, and Janet L. Surrey. 1991, 29.

[115] Gray John. 1993. *What You Feel You Can Heal. A Guide for Enriching Relationships.* London, Pan Macmillan, p. 10.

more accessible. Living at a close-range lead to familiarity. Individuals begin to see they have similar ideas and values in common and therefore attraction is strengthened. Proximity leads to the discovery of certain similarities among individuals. For, the more people spend time together, the more they discover they have things in common. Gerrig and Zimbardo affirm that "similarity on dimensions such as beliefs, attitudes, and values foster friendship[116]". People who are similar to another in these aspects provide a sense of personal validation.

Contrary to many psychologists that maintain that similarity facilitates attraction, Grey maintains that "we are drawn to this person not because they are similar to us but because they are different. Our soulmate embodies qualities and attributes that we unconsciously seek to find within ourselves[117]". Awareness of the differences between people is a major prerequisite of love. It is what one lacks that attracts one in the other. The challenge is to understand, accept, and appreciate those differences, and then they will naturally emerge in the other person. In fact, the author insists that intense attraction is a manifestation of an unconscious difference in the other. This creates conflict and ignites a strong urge for imitation and identification in friendship.

To handle the distractions associated with attractions towards a person, especially the opposite sex, the fundamental thing is to propose a more attractive alternative. This helps to resist the temptations posed by attraction. A deep understanding of commitment in the psychological sense of the word is helpful. That is, commitment as "partner's intentions to stay in relationships, pledges of loyalty or devotion, or feelings of connectedness[118]". So that a priest or a religious makes a choice and decision to be loyal in her relationship

---

[116] Gerrig, Richard J., and Phillip G. Zimbardo. 2010, 532.

[117] Gray John. 1993, p. 12.

[118] Forgas, Joseph P., and Julie Fitness. 2008. *Social Relationships. Cognitive, Affective, and Motivational Processes*. NY: Psychology Press Taylor and Francis Group, p. 47.

with Christ with great intensity. Also, imagining derogatory attractive alternatives reduces the attraction. Imagining the future Bridegroom and contemplating His love and care, writing one's love story or journal and recounting the favours one has received helps one to be committed to the Lord.

COMMUNICATION DYNAMICS AND PROCESSES

Communication is vital to any group or interpersonal setting. The quality of communication determines the quality of relationship of the group. Through it, members influence one another either positively or negatively. Good communication enhances good responses. Argyle emphasizes that non-verbal communication (which ranges from facial expression, gaze, voice and gestures) is a powerful means which influences people's response and behaviour. He believes that non-verbal communication has more weight than spoken words. According to him, all social signals are encoded and decoded by a sender and a receiver thus: Sender –encodes –Signal ---decodes – receiver. In non-verbal communication, the unconscious plays a very significant role. Often the sender is unaware of the message he or she is sending across. It sends emotions and attitudes to people. The face is fundamental to communication as it indicates emotional reactions. It also communicates attitudes such as likes, dislikes and hostility. The face expresses the emotional states like happiness, surprise, fear, sadness, anger, disgust or contempt. However, some of these facial expressions are not necessarily because of emotions, some are cognitively motivated.

Non-verbal communication not only provides information, it modulates interaction, expresses the level of relationship, takes into consideration the social-cultural context and harmonizes the content and the process. Some gestures like smiles communicates love and acceptance and decrease the presence of negative and unpleasant emotions. It creates conducive atmosphere for all to participate in the interaction, thereby decreasing psychological distance among individuals.

Fisher believes as well that there is no verbal communication without non-verbal communication. His research shows that non-verbal communication carries about 65% of the information in a discussion[119]. The emphasis is in combining both. Gaze is central to interpersonal relationship. It creates an avenue for the reception of another person's non-verbal signals, especially the facial expression. Eye contact is the most crucial aspect of gaze. Mutual gaze is an important social signal for liking. However, eye contact can also be unpleasant and embarrassing if there is too much of it and if mutual glances are too long. This is because it may generate some levels of physiological arousal. It can be distractive and adds to cognitive overload. On the other hand, the tone of voice communicates more. While a happy person speaks in a clear and pure tone, a depressed or displeased fellow speaks slowly, at a low pitch, with many break-ages in voice. There is no fluency and eloquence in the person's speech.

A very important aspect of communication is empathic listen-ing, that is listening with full attention. A situation whereby a person is speaking and the other engages in another thing while listening, disturbs the psyche of the speaker. Even with the assurance of some phrases like "go on, I can hear you", sends a message of 'distur-bance' or 'rejection'. Listening is not a passive act, it is also active. The same principle of Stephen Covey holds here: *seek first to under-stand, then to be understood.* Most people listen only in the techni-cal sense of the word, so that when one is speaking, they are either preparing to interrupt or to counteract or to make their own input. Constant projection is against effective communication. Listening deeply gives the room to understand the tremendous differences in interpretation and perception of concepts by people.

Furthermore, we cannot ignore the influence of the modern communication system of the present society. Almost every adult is

---

[119] Fisher, Simon E., Ludin Jawed, Steve Williams, Ibrahim A. Dekha, Richard Smith, and Williams Sue. 2000. *Working with Conflicts. Skills and Strate-gies for Action.* NY: Zed Books, p. 112.

computer literate today. Most children and teenagers are 'digital natives'[120]. Its pervasiveness in our lives cannot be overlooked, nor can the great positive influence be ignored. Communicating in computer-mediated context is a type of communication which has helped so much in disseminating even the gospel message, especially when immediate communication is not possible, although immediate communication is the best as one transmits the message more directly. Too much mediation may be either as a defense mechanism to avoid a person or some issues. This breeds bureaucracy and leads to relational and social collapse.

Because priests and religious are to work or are working among the 'digital natives', they also need to learn the dynamics and logistics of the modern means of communication. The biggest concern and challenge are the impact it has on pastoral ministry and relational life, of which the greatest challenge lies in the quick and immediate dissemination of false and incomplete information.

CONFLICT MANAGEMENT AND RESOLUTION

Some priests and religious suffer adversities in silence. Some are afraid of sharing their difficulties with others to avoid more complications. Most can handle their difficulties and challenges. Apart from some inevitable problems like sickness, loss of a dear one or loss of job, most problems can be prevented or resolved. The question of incompatibility is a reality, but the self-donation to Christ and humanity must transcend this concept of incompatibility. Love must transcend hatred, cooperation and appreciation must transcend incompatibility.

---

[120] Palgrey and Gasser refer to those born after 1980 as the 'digital natives'. Digital natives are constantly connected. They have a network of friends and acquaintances. They possess tremendous skills which can be frightening and even intimidating to the 'digital migrants'. The World Wide Web made browsing easier and more accessible. The World Wide Web (www) which makes browsing easier and more accessible is their very good companion. They care less about privacy as they spend so much time online and prudence is not their strong point.

Covey emphasises the need to change one's mentality or paradigm in other to solve daily problems. It's about cognitive flexibility. Every conflict has two possibilities or sides to it and each of these is rooted in a paradigm. Paradigm here refers to "a pattern or model of thinking that influences how we behave. It is like a map that helps us decide which direction to go. The map we see, determines what we do, and what we do determines the results we get. If we shift paradigms, our behaviour and results change as well[121]". No map is perfect.

In every conflict or misunderstanding, two outstanding mental maps are involved. That is, my mental map, and your own. The problem is in individual believing that their own map is not complete and perfect and therefore to combine both. Covey suggests that the moment both parties realize that their perspectives are not all that correct and complete, they look for what he calls "the 3rd alternative". In this the principle of synergy becomes indispensable. Synergy is what happens when two or more respectful human beings determine together to go beyond their preconceived ideas to meet a great challenge. It's about the passion, the energy and the ingenuity of creating a new reality that is far better than the old reality[122]. Synergy is beyond mere resolving a conflict. It goes further to embrace a new way which is more inclusive and beneficial to individuals. There is a kind of intermingling that strengthens the new perspective.

In every conflict, it is good to try to seek the middle ground. The defence mechanism of splitting whereby people understand issues as "either/or", black or white is not helpful for reconciliation. Polarization is often a block to conflict resolution. Unconditional positive regard for the other helps people to believe that the other person has a point he or she wishes to make, and therefore should be listened to. Dialogue helps in the resolution of every conflict. Both should search for a corporate solution. What do we do?

---

[121] Covey Stephen. 2011. *The 3rd Alternative: Solving Life's Most Difficult Problems*. NY: Free Press, p. 10.

[122] Covey Stephen. 2011, p. 12.

Conflict is inevitable in any group. In fact, the absence of conflict will suggest a passive peace in any group. This will further imply a superficial relationship with people. A functional family or community is not one without any problem or inconvenience, it is not also a place where everything works out perfectly, but a place where people are willing and disposed to seek for solution always. The two major conflict in religious communities are conflict of need and that of value. These preferences create conflict. Fisher et al, note that differences in values and viewpoints can cause conflict, but at the same time are often very enriching. Differences in values, principles, likes, perspectives are inevitable. They bring disagreement, yet they unite and enrich people in relationship. There is no point suppressing conflicts as they lead to future problems in a more pronounced manner. Conflicts mean there are two or more individuals or groups whose goals or visions are incompatible. However, they lead to a deeper understanding of oneself and the group. For a group, it brings a kind of re-structuring and re-wiring to achieve an improved situation. But individuals must be disposed to do this.

Although the Bible says, forgive one another as soon as a quarrel begins (Cf. Col.3:13); the sunset must not find you still angry (Cf. Eph. 4: 26), it is always good to analyse a conflict. The purpose is to help the person answer some soul-searching questions like: *How did I contribute to the present conflict? How could I have done it better?* Analysing helps one to find the cause of the conflict and subsequently aids in the solution. Conflicts should be addressed as soon as they arise. The goal is for the individual or the group to proceed towards a relationship in which they can develop their greatest potential. Conflict blocks this development. It impedes collaboration. To resolve conflict, there is the need to define the problem, diagnose the causes, generate possible solution, decide on a mutually acceptable solution and implement the solution within a time limit. All these are to be integrated for a better solution.

Different strategies ranging from conflict prevention, which aims at preventing the outbreak of disagreement; conflict settlement which aims at ending the violent behaviour by reaching a peace

118

agreement; conflict management which aims at limiting and avoiding future violence by promoting positive behavioural changes in
the parties involved; conflict resolution which addresses the causes
of conflict and seeks to build new and lasting relationships between
hostile groups[123]. Creating a new reality is based on giving importance to the relationship existing between the individuals. So that
each person gives up his or her own way, tries to imbibe part of the
other person's way for the sake of their existing relationship.

---

[123] Fisher, Simon E., Ludin Jawed, Steve Williams, Ibrahim A. Dekha, Richard Smith, and Williams Sue. 2000, p. 7.

Chapter Six

WAYS OF SUSTAINING AFFECTIVE MATURITY

SUSTAINING AFFECTIVE MATURITY THROUGH PSYCHOTHERAPY SESSIONS

Technically speaking, psychotherapy is "both an art and a science[124]". It literally means *treatment for the mind*. It originates from the psychoanalysis of Freud, it is a kind of *talking cure*. It is geared towards a treatment which is conducted by a trained professional (psychotherapist), within a set framework in order to improve the mental and emotional health of a patient or the individual in question. The empirical data from different psychological tests and interviews provide the best therapeutic techniques to be applied. Psychotherapy is geared towards helping people to learn some constructive ways of dealing with their challenges and difficulties in life. Sometimes, it is mainly supportive as in the case of aiding people to handle their different traumatic experiences. Some versions of psychodynamic psychotherapy concentrate on solving the client's immediate problem, and in this case, it becomes goal-oriented. Therefore, it offers some suggestions on the adoption of some coping mechanisms. Through it, people learn to understand and control themselves better.

The goals of psychotherapy are to "relieve patient's emotional distress, assist them in finding solution to problems in their lives, and helping them modify personality characteristics and behavior patterns that are preventing them from realizing their potential for productive work and rewarding interpersonal relationships[125]".

---

[124] Weiner, Irving B., and Robert F. Bornstein. 2009. *Principles of Psychotherapy. Promoting Evidence-Based Psychodynamic Practice*. Third Edition. Hoboken, NJ: John Wiley & Sons, p. vii-ix.

[125] Weiner, Irving B., and Robert F. Bornstein. 2009, p. 8.

Apart from many problems caused by environmental circumstances or by the idiosyncratic nature of others, there are psychological problems which individuals must confront. This makes them anxious and therefore more disposed to benefit from the relief offered by psychotherapy. During psychotherapy, the clients are encouraged to express their thoughts and feelings without minding how important or meaningful they appear to be. Openness and transparency during sessions yield swift fruit and progress. It provides the opportunity for one to examine and carefully evaluate one's experiences, conflicts and challenges and to see how one contributed to it. It opens a dynamism of healing procedure. The aim is to foster some level of autonomy and interdependence as well among people.

Psychodynamic psychotherapy is more adaptable and recommended for priests and religious. It means *mind in motion*. As believed that an individual is affected by the unconscious, and that the elements in the unconscious affect conscious thoughts, feelings, and behavior[126]. The aim of this is to help priests and religious to understand the elements of the unconscious that are affecting their conscious thoughts, feelings and behavior. When they gain insight about this, they can work and deal with the basic problems associated with them (memories, conflicts, erroneous perceptions, dysfunctional relationships etc.), and then process them.

It has been observed that some priests and religious are psychologically distressed. This sometimes leads to psychosomatic sicknesses, so that one becomes a perpetual patient without any clear diagnosis from the doctor. This is because some sicknesses are caused by internal agency (anxiety, phobia) rather than external agency. They battle with different unacceptable aspects of the self. Often, there are many contradictory and opposing forces which people are faced with in life. It is no surprise that one's internal desires often

---

[126] Cabaniss, Deborah L. and Sabrina Cherry, Carolyn Douglas and Anna Schwartz, 2013. *Psychodynamic Psychotherapy. A Clinical Manual.* Wiley-Blackwell Publishers, p. 3-5.

conflict with spiritual, moral and ethical code of conducts. These attractive desires which are incompatible with one's proclaimed values are clarified and processed during psychotherapy sessions. Through psychotherapy, priests and religious can learn their psychodynamics, how they function in daily life and why they function that way. This helps them to acquire and use the adaptive mechanisms and consequently reduce excessive and inappropriate use of defense mechanism. Again, it gives them room to process many childhood hurts, traumas, emotional problems and other forms of frustrations which inhibit their developmental journey towards affective maturity.

SUSTAINING AFFECTIVE MATURITY THROUGH RESILIENCE

Resilience "is the capacity to bounce back from setbacks and move ahead"[127]. It gives one the room to persevere even in the midst of many disappointments and setbacks. It is that capacity to sustain especially emotional injury without being stabilized. Many experiences can destabilize the celibate; annual postings, well prepared pastoral visit which ends up by the bishop sending his secretary, frustrated ambition for further studies etc. Resilience implies that, despite these disappointments[128], the person still moves on with courage and positive attitude. Resiliency returns the whole body to its homeostasis after distasteful experiences and prevents psychic damage. While many people are from good, happy, peaceful and in fact functional families, most are from dysfunctional families. These include divorce, separated, single-parent etc. By every standard this breeds unpleasant experiences which manifest in different ways in life. It is the power of resilience that prevents people of this sort from breaking down emotionally.

Resilient people can integrate their difficulties and interpret them as challenges which provide opportunities for growth and maturity.

---

[127] Parappully Jose and Jose Kuttianimattatthil. 2012, p.105.

[128] NON C'É NOTA

122

> *We must never forget that we may also find meaning in life even when confronted with a hopeless situation, when facing a fate that cannot be changed.*
>
> VICTOR FRANKL

When one survives a difficult experience, one masters oneself the more and acquires more techniques for future experiences. It gives room for creativity. In the Article, *Disadvantage, Resilience and Human Maturity*, Thannickal outlined some characteristics of resilient people. According to him, capacity to face reality, to find meaning in one's life and to be creative are the most common characteristic among resilient people. In them, their sense of reality is not impaired or distorted. They accept the ups and downs of life and put in their best to transform it into their dreams and goal. When they fail, they accept that fact. Again, resilient people appreciate their daily life experiences and find meaning in them. Victor Frankl advices that "we must never forget that we may also find meaning in life even when confronted with a hopeless situation, when facing a fate that cannot be changed"[129]. Adherence to spiritual and ethical values help boost one's capacity for resilience.

The following fifteen points of Thannickal can be of help to priests and religious as they strive to build and develop the power of resilience:

- Develop a *positive view of the self* with emotional balance. Explore issues of identity, identification and socialisation focusing on dealing with discriminatory experiences and challenging stereotypes.

- Reframe *personal narratives*. Tell your story emphasizing the redemptive aspects that have developed the story further.

- Instil *social concern*, altruism and generativity. Have the desire to pass on a future that is better than the one we had, to the next generation.

---

[129] Frankl Victor E. 2005. *Man's Search for Meaning*. NY: Washington Square Press, p. 116.

- Learn how to live a *meaningful life* in a variety of circumstances.

- Practice *optimism, blending it with strong levels of realism,* with the ability to confront reality.

- Have a *mentor*. Identify possibly a resilient role model, someone who is known and who inspires.

- Establish a supportive social *network*.

- Develop a *moral compass* and unbreakable *beliefs* in God, ideals and principles that help one to transcend oneself. Become aware of the positive value of pluralism, and learn to find one's place within in.

- Develop acceptance and *cognitive flexibility*, the ability to adapt one's knowledge and thinking to new situations.

- Develop the *motivation to be effective* in life, work hard, but also well.

- Work hard at *academic achievement*. It is one sure-fire method to climb out of early handicaps.

- Develop *humour*. Laugh as much as one can.

- Stay *physically* fit. Watch out for balanced diets rich in carbohydrates, and proteins.

- *Pray one's histories*. Bring the figures and situations of the past life, with their possible consequences, and potentials into one's prayer.

- *Identify a talent* and develop it assiduously. Learn it, use it, and become creative in it[130].

---

[130] Thannickal Joseph. 2012. "Disadvantage, Resilience and Human Maturity", *in Psychosexual Integration and Celibate Maturity*, p. 137.

RECOURSE TO THE BLESSED VIRGIN MARY, MOTHER OF GOOD COUNSEL

A true Marian devotion is the secret of sustaining one's all round growth and maturity in life. I do not intend the devotees who are more inclined to the externals and outward appearances, multiplying confraternities, prayers and so on, recite as many rosaries as possible. It consists in priests and religious who have high esteem for the Mother of God, and who are grateful for the privilege to be called daughters and sons of Mary. This sense of gratitude begets great admiration of Her and therefore instills a strong attraction to Her virtues. When a priest or religious attains this height of great admiration, identification and internalization of her virtues takes place. At this stage, one imitates them and tries to be Marylike, so that in most life circumstances one is confronted with the question, what will Mary do in this situation, how would she handle a situation like this? It helps one to develop confidence in Her, so that before Her, the celibate remains a child in the mum's arms who is sure of the mother's warmth and affection. It is this confidence that compels one to go back to Her even in the weakest and darkest moment of one's life.

Again, by consistent imitation of the principal virtues of Mary, priests and religious will be perfecting themselves and gaining more resilience. Her outstanding capacity and virtue of pondering is of great importance to the concept of affective maturity. Pondering here should not only be understood from the reflective point of view, or in the Greek sense of Socrates, *unexamined life is not worth living*. It is rather more in the Hebrew sense of meaning "to hold, carry, and transform tension so as not to give it back in kind, knowing that whatever energies we do not transform we will transmit[131]". It is this virtue that provides the priest or religious the graceful opportunity for 'working through', a kind of introspection on one's personal life and experiences. It helps one to contain his or her feelings, explore

---

[131] Rolheiser, Ronald. 2014. *Sacred Fire. A Vision for a Deeper Human and Christian Maturity*. NY: Image, p. 147.

them and digest them. This virtue prevents one from exploding even at the height of stress. It strengthens one's capacity for impulse control.

Total confidence in Mary is helpful. She directs and accompanies one like a good mother. She steadies one when he or she is about to fall and lifts one up when one falls. She reproves one like a charitable mother, and sometimes she even chastises his or her[132]. Confidence in Her implies meditative prayer and listening to her inspirations, her counsels and advices. What could be more fulfilling than having a tender mother like Her?

---

[132] Louis-Marie Gregnion De Monfort, 2010. *True Devotion to Mary with Preparation for Total Consecration*, p. 111.

CONCLUSION

To acquire affective maturity, there is the need to understand the psychological structures and dynamics of the 'self'. We intend here, the self that is not enslaved by the unconscious or the past, but the human person in the present. That is the person that remembers the past with gratitude to God and ready to make amends for the future where it is necessary. In other words, the self as the subject who actively experiences, perceives, feels, imagines, chooses, remembers or plans. Affective maturity extends the invitation to all to observe, elaborate, understand, internalize and own up the complexities of the human heart. It gives room for integration of the different polarities and to avoid splitting; either white or black, either good or bad, but to embrace the law of inclusion (both). When one is in touch with oneself and recognizes one's own complexities, the sensitivity and vulnerability of the hearts, one is moved by empathy which gives birth to forgiveness.

When we are affectively mature, we can accept reality as it is without much animosities and grievances in our hearts, we can accept our histories, understand our past as a contribution to our present life in view of a brighter future, we can process our loses and regrets and understand ourselves better. It disposes us for the capacity for change, both a change of heart and a change in attitude and behavior. Self-confidence is necessary in order to strike a balance between autonomy and dependence. Over dependence suggests that others are superior to us and it kills one's initiative.

The most important questions in the concept of developing the self in affective maturity should be: "Who am I in relation to the changing streams of emotions, thoughts and perceptions within? What do I really want when confronted with the tension between my needs, attitudes and values, and the expectations and demands of my environment?"[133]. The priest or religious must be one capable of asserting his or her feelings and emotions. An affectively mature priest or religious is not one who is cold and inexpressive for fear of making mistakes, but one who has mastered to an extent the relational skills in handling and expressing his or her emotions in a responsible manner. Awareness of one's limitations in this area is also to be recognized, leaving space for growth and further development. Affective maturity is a great asset in the development of emotional and mental potentials which renders one more productive in the use and exercise of one's talents, gifts and personalities. With this, it fulfills one's needs and disposes one to approach God through others in responsible relationships. This in effect fosters our spiritual maturity, that is, the capacity to establish and enter a deeper and personal relationship with God.

In all, affective maturity does not therefore mean that one reaches a stage in life where he or she is no longer aware of any tensions and conflicts within oneself, or crave for affection and love, but rather that the individual develops a better and an integrated approach to all these. After all, every human person is always at the state of becoming. In the different phases of becoming there comes growth as every experience is an opportunity for the self to grow. "For the self is not seen today as a monolithic unity which one 'possesses' once and for all. Rather the self has to be acquired in an ongoing process of integration, which connects cognitive, affective and operational or active aspects with each other"[134]. The grandiose fantasies of achieving wholeness and holiness can become frustrating, disappointing. Accepting the different stages or seasons in one's life together their peculiar challenges is an enormous task. This has serious implications regarding the way we view what affective maturity requires of us.

---

[133] Manenti, Alessandro., Stefano Guarinelli, and Hans Zollner. 2007, p. 47.

[134] Manenti, Alessandro., Stefano Guarinelli, and Hans Zollner. 2007, p. 64.

BIBLIOGRAPHY

AA. VV. *The African Bible*. 1999. Nairobi, Kenya: Paulines Publications.

ALPER, GUNEY M. 2006. *The Guilt and Morality Functions*. Naperville, ILL: Sourcebooks Inc.

ALPORT, GORDON W. 1961. *Pattern and Growth in Personality*. NY: Holt, Rinehart & Winston.

ARNOLD, MAGDA B. 1969. "Human Emotion and Action". Pp. 54-60 in *Human Action. Conceptual and Empirical Issues*, edited by T. Mitchel. NY: Academic Press.

ARNOLD, MAGDA B. 1970. *Feelings and Emotions*. NY: Academic Press.

ARON, ARTHUR., and ELAINE N. ARON. 1986. *Love and the Expansion of Self. Understanding Attraction and Satisfaction*. NY: Hemisphere Publishing Corporation.

AU, WILKIE., and NOREEN CANNON. 1995. *Urgings of The Heart. A Spirituality of Integration*. NY: Paulist Press.

AUSUBEL, DAVID P.1959. *Theory and Problems of Child Development*. NY: Grune and Stratton.

BANDURA, ALBEIT. 1997. *Self-Efficacy: The Exercise of Control*. NY: Freeman.

BARRETT, FELDMAN LISA, LEWIS MICHAEL, and M. JEANNETTE HAVILAND-JONES. 2016. *Handbook of Emotions*. Fourth Edition. NY: Guilford Press.

BAUMEISTER, ROY F. 1993. *Self-Esteem. The Puzzle of Low Self-Regard*. NY: Plenum Press.

BELSKY, JAY, and TERESA NEZWORSKI. 1998. *Clinical Implications of Attachment*. NJ: Lawrence Erbaum Associates Publishers.

BOWLBY, JOHN E. 1979. *The Making and Breaking of Affectional Bonds*. London, U.K.: Tavistock.

BRANDEN, NATHANIEL. 2001. *The Psychology of Self-Esteem: A Revolutionary Approach to Self-Understanding that Launched a New Era in Modern Psychology*. San Francisco, CA: Jossey-Bass.

CABANISS, DEBORAH L., and SABRINA CHERRY, CAROLYN DOUGLAS and ANNA SCHWARTZ, 2013. *Psychodynamic Psychotherapy. A Clinical Manual*. Wiley-Blackwell Publishers.

CENCINI, AMAEDO R. 1998. *The Sentiments of the Son. A Formative Journey in Consecrated Life*. Bologna, Italia: Centro Editoriale Dehoniano.

CENCINI, AMAEDO R. 2009. *Virginity and Celibacy Today*. Nairobi, Kenya: Paulines Publications.

CENCINI, AMAEDO, and ALESSANDRO MANENTI. 2010. *Psychology and Formation: Structures and Dynamics*. Mumbai, India: Pauline Sisters.

COLEMAN, G. D. 1992. *Human Sexuality: An all-embracing Gift*. NY: Alba House.

COLMAN, ANDREW M. 2009. *Oxford Dictionary of Psychology*. NY: Oxford University Press.

CRAIN, WILLIAM. 2005. *Theories of Development: Concepts and Applications*. NY: Pearson Education, Inc.

DAVIDSON, RICHARD J., KLAUS R. SCHERER, and HILL H. GOLDSMITH. 2003. *The Handbook of Affective Sciences*. NY: Oxford University Press.

DECI, EDWARD L., and RICHARD M. RYAN. 1995. "Human Autonomy: The Basis for True Self-Esteem". Pp. 31-46 in *Efficacy, Agency, and Self-Esteem*, edited by M. H. Kernis. NY: Plenum Press.

DEAUX, KAY., and MARIANNE LAFRANCE. 1998. *"Gender"*. Pp.788-827 in *Handbook of Social Psychology*. Vol.2, edited by T. Gilbert, S. T Fiske and G. Lindzey. Boston. MA: McGraw-Hill.

ELLISON, CAROL R. 2000. *Women's Sexualities. Generations of Women Share Intimate Secrets of Sexual Self-Acceptance*. Oakland, CA: New Harbinger Publications.

FISHER, SIMON E., LUDIN JAWED, STEVE WILLIAMS, IBRAHIM A. DEKHA, RICHARD SMITH, and WILLIAMS SUE. 2000. *Working with Conflicts. Skills and Strategies for Action*. NY: Zed Books.

FORGAS, JOSEPH P., and JULIE FITNESS. 2008. *Social Relationships. Cognitive, Affective, and Motivational Processes*. NY: Psychology Press Taylor and Francis Group.

FRANKL, VICTOR E. *Man's Search for Meaning*. 2005. NY: Washington Square Press.

GERRIG, RICHARD J., and PHILLIP G. ZIMBARDO. 2010. *Psychology and Life*. Nineteenth Edition. Boston, MA: Pearson.

GOLEMAN, DANIEL. 2005. *Emotional Intelligence. The 10th Anniversary Edition*. NY: Bantam Dell.

GORDON, CHAD, and KENNETH. J. GERGEN. 1968. *The Self in Social Interaction*. Vol. I. NY: John Willey and Sons.

HARMON-JONES, EDDIE., and CINDY HARMON-JONES. 2016. "Anger". Pp. 774- 787 in *Handbook of Emotions*, edited by F. L. Barrett., M. Lewis and J.M. Haviland-Jones. Fourth Edition. NY: Guilford Press.

HOGG, MICHAEL A., and SCOTT TINDALE. 2001. *Blackwell Handbook of Social Psychology: Group Processes*. Malden, MA: Blackwell Publishers Inc.

HOGG, MICHAEL A., and JOEL COOPER. 2007. *The Sage Handbook of Social Psychology*. Concise Student Edition. London, U.K.: Sage Publications.

HOGG, MICHAEL A., and GRAHAM M. VAUGHAN. 2011. *Social Psychology*. Sixth Edition. London, U.K.: Pearson Press.

HOYLE, RICK H. 2010. *Handbook of Personality and Self-Regulation*. Oxford, U.K.: Blackwell Publishing Ltd.

IMODA, FRANCO. 2007. *Human Development. Psychology and Mystery*. Leuven, Belgium: Peeters.

IZAD, CARROLLE E., JEROME KEGAN, and ROBERT B. ZAJONC. 1982. *Emotions, Cognition and Behaviour*. London, U.K.: Cambridge University Press.

JORDAN, JUDITH V., ALEXANDRA G. KAPLAN, JEAN B. MILLER, IRENE P. STIVER, and JANET L. SURREY. 1991. *Women's Growth in Connection: Writings from the Stone Center*. NY: Guilford Press.

KIELY, BARTHOLOMEW M. 1987. *Psychology and Moral Theology*. Rome, Italy: Gregorian University Press.

LEARY, MARK R., and JUNE P. TANGNEY. 2003. *Handbook of Self and Identity*. NY: Guilford Press.

LEDOUX, JOSEPH. 2003. *Synaptic Self: How Our Brains Become Who We Are*. NY: Penguin.

LEVINSON, DAVID., JAMES J. PONZETTI, and PETER F. JORGENSEN. 1999. *Encyclopaedia of Human Emotions*. Vol.1. NY: Macmillan.

LEVINSON, DAVID., JAMES J PONZETTI, and PETER F JORGENSEN. 1999. *Encyclopaedia of Human Emotions*. Vol.2, NY: Macmillan.

LEWIS, MICHAEL, JEANNETTE M. HAVILAND-JONES, and LISA. F. BARRETT. 2008. *Hand Book of Emotions*. NY: Guilford Press.

LOPEZ, SHANE J., and CHARLES R. SNYDER. 2007. *Positive Psychology. The Scientific and Practical Explorations of Human Strengths*. Oaks, CA: Sage Publications.

LOUIS-MARIE GREGNION DE MONFORT, 2010. *True Devotion to Mary with Preparation for Total Consecration*, p. 111.

MANENTI, ALESSANDRO, STEFANO GUARINELLI, and HANS ZOLLNER. 2007. *Formation and the Person: Essays on Theory and Practice*. Leuven, Belgium: Peeters Press.

MATSUMOTO, DAVID. 2009. *The Cambridge Dictionary of Psychology*. NY: Cambridge University Press.

MCLAREN, KARLA. 2010. *The Language of Emotions. What Your Feelings are Trying to Tell You*. Louisville, CO: Sounds True, Inc.

MEEKS, LINDA and HEIT, PHILIP. 2001. *Sexuality and Character Education K-12*. Chicago, Every day learning Corporation.

MULLANEY, BRENNAN J. 2008. *Authentic Love. Theory and Therapy*. NY: Society of St. Paul.

NICHOLS, MICHAEL P. 2010. *Family Therapy. Concepts and Methods*. Ninth Edition. NY: Pearson.

PARAPPULLY, JOSE and JOSE KUTTIANIMATTATHIL. 2012. Psychosexual Integration and Celibate Maturity. Handbook for Religious and Priestly Formation. Vol. 1&2. Salesian Psychological Association, India, Bangalore

PECK, SCOTT M. 2003. *The Road Less Travelled. A New Psychology of Love, Traditional Values and Spiritual Growth. 25th Anniversary Edition*. NY: Touchstone.

ROTHBART, MARY K., and ROSARIO M. RUEDA. 2005. "The Development of Effortful Control". Pp. 167-180 in *Developing Individuality in the Human Brain: A Tribute to Michael I. Posner,* edited by E. Mayr and S. Keele. Washington, D.C.: American Psychological Association.

ROGERS, CARL R. 1951. *Client-Centered Therapy. Its Current Practice, Implications, and Theory*.

CAMBRIDGE, MA. Houghton Mifflin Company.

ROGERS, CARL R. 1961. *On Becoming a Person. A Psychotherapist's View of Psychotherapy*, NY: Houghton Mifflin Company.

ROLHEISER, RONALD. 2014. *Sacred Fire. A Vision for a Deeper Human and Christian Maturity*. NY: Image.

RULLA, LUIGI M. 2004. *Anthropology of Christian Vocation*. Vol. 1. Rome, Italy: Gregorian University Press.

SAINT LOUIS-MARIE GREGNION DE MONFORT, 2010. *True Devotion to Mary with Preparation for Total Consecration*.

SCHAFFER, DAVID R. and KATHERINE KIPP. 2010. *Developmental Psychology: Childhood and Adolescence*. Eight Edition. Belmont, VA: Wadsworth Cenage Learning.

SCHNEIDERS, SANDRA M. 2000. *Finding the Treasure. Locating Catholic Religious Life in a New Ecclesial and Cultural Context*. NJ: Paulist Press.

SCHNEIDERS, SANDRA M. 2001. *Selling All. Commitment, Consecrated Celibacy, and Community in Catholic Religious Life*. NJ: Paulist Press.

SCHNEIDERS, SANDRA M. 2013. *Buying the Field. Catholic Religious Life in Mission to the World*. NY: Paulist Press.

SIEGEL, DANIEL J. 1999. *The Developing Mind: How Relationships and the Brain Interact to Shape Who We Are*. NY: Guildford Press.

SIPE, RICHARD, A. W. 1996. *Celibacy: A way of loving, Living and Serving*. Liguori, MO: Triumph Books.

SPITZBERG, BRIAN H., and WILLIAM R. CUPACH. 2010. *The Dark Side of Close Relationships*. NY: Lawrence Erlbaum Associates Publishers.

STRONGMAN, KENNETH T. 2003. *The Psychology of Emotion. From Everyday Life to Theory*. Fifth Edition. Chichester, U.K.: John Wiley and Sons Press.

WEINER, IRVING B., and ROBERT F. BORNSTEIN. 2009. *Principles of Psychotherapy. Promoting Evidence-Based Psychodynamic Practice*. Third Edition. Hoboken, NJ: John Wiley & Sons, Inc.

WILDE, JERRY. 1996. Treating Anger, Anxiety, and Depression in Children and Adolescents. A Cognitive Behavioral Perspective. Philadelphia, PA: Accelerated Development.

WITTBERG, PATRICIA S. 2012. *Building Strong Church Communities: A Sociological Overview*. Mahwah, NJ: Paulist Press

ARTICLES

ASCHENBRENNER, GEORGE A. 1985. "Celibacy in Community and Ministry". Pp. 27-33 in *Human Development*, Vol.6.

DEWALD, P.A. 1994. "Principles of Supportive Psychotherapy". Pp.505-518 in *American Journal of Psychotherapy,* Vol. 48.

IOANNIDOU, F., and V. KONSTANTIKAKI. 2008. "Empathy and Emotional Intelligence: What is it Really About?". Pp. 118-123 in *International Journal of Caring Sciences*, Sept-Dec. Vol. 1.

MUKUNDAN, C.R 2016. "Assigning Meaning to Emotional Arousal". *The International Journal of Indian Psychology*. Vol.3: Issue July: N0. 61.

UMOREN, LINUS. 2012. "Human Sexuality: Crisis and Challenges in Formation". Pp.55-86 in *The Catholic Voyage. A Publication of the Conference of Major Superiors of Nigeria*, Vol. 9.

RAHNER K. 1967. "Lettera aperta sul celibate". Uitgever, Brescia, P.18.

WANNER, R. 1987. *Aelred of Rievaulx: Twelfth Century Answers to Twentieth Century Questions*. Review for Religious, 46 (6), p. 923.

INDEX

LITOGRAFIA LEBERIT
Via Aurelia, 308   00165 ROMA
Tel. e Fax 06.6620695